PERGAMON INSTITUTE OF ENGLISH
(OXFORD)

Position Papers

ESP (ENGLISH FOR SPECIFIC PURPOSES)

ESP

(ENGLISH FOR SPECIFIC PURPOSES):
the present position

PAULINE C ROBINSON
Centre for Applied Language Studies
University of Reading

PERGAMON PRESS
Oxford · New York · Toronto · Sydney · Paris · Frankfurt

UK	Pergamon Press Ltd, Headington Hill Hall, Oxford, OX3 0BW, England
USA	Pergamon Press Inc, Maxwell House, Fairview Park, Elmsford, New York 10523, USA
CANADA	Pergamon of Canada, Suite 104, 150 Consumers Road, Willowdale, Ontario M2J 1P9, Canada
AUSTRALIA	Pergamon Press (Aust) Pty Ltd, PO Box 544, Potts Point, NSW 2011, Australia
FRANCE	Pergamon Press SARL, 24 rue des Ecoles, 75240 Paris, Cedex 05, France
FEDERAL REPUBLIC OF GERMANY	Pergamon Press GmBH, 6242 Kronberg-Taunus, Pferdstrasse 1, Federal Republic of Germany

Copyright © 1980 Pergamon Press Ltd.

All rights reserved. No part of this publication may be reproduced, stored in a retrieval system or transmitted in any form by any means: electronic, electrostatic, magnetic tape, mechanical, photocopying, recording or otherwise, without permission in writing from the publishers.

First edition 1980

British Library Cataloguing in Publication Data

Robinson, Pauline C
   ESP (English for Specific Purposes).
   (Pergamon Institute of English (Oxford).
   Position papers).
   1. English language – Study and teaching –
   Foreign students
   I. Title
   428'.2'407   PE1128A2   79–41105

   ISBN 0–08–024585–4 flexicover

*Printed in Great Britain
at The Pitman Press, Bath*

Contents

	Page
Preface	vii
Introduction	1
1. Definitions of ESP	5
2. Survey of theoretical positions	15
2.1 Historical survey of ESP	15
2.2 Register analysis	16
2.3 Discourse analysis and the communicative approach	20
2.4 Student motivation and the analysis of needs	26
2.5 Syllabus design	31
2.6 Materials production	34
2.7 Methodology	38
2.8 Generalizability of materials	40
3. Analysis of current publications	43
3.1 Survey of what is available	43
3.2 Summary of the main features of the available textbooks	44
3.3 Series of books	45
3.3/1 English for Careers	45
3.3/2 English in Focus	46
3.3/3 English for Special Purposes	49
3.3/4 English Studies	50
3.3/5 Nucleus	51
3.3/6 Special English	54
3.3/7 Materials produced by ELTDU	54

3.4	Textbooks on Social Science topics	56
3.5	Textbooks on the Physical Sciences	57
3.6	Textbooks on Technology	61
3.7	Textbooks on Medicine	63
3.8	Textbooks on commercial topics	66
3.9	Materials for study skills or EAP	67
3.10	Concluding remarks	70
	3.10/1 The communicative approach	70
	3.10/2 Grammar	70
	3.10/3 Vocabulary	71
	3.10/4 Reading	71
	3.10/5 ESP and ELT	73

Appendix I	Implications for teacher training	75
Appendix II	Testing and evaluation	79
Appendix III	Self-directed learning and self-assessment	85
Bibliography		93

Note

Numbers in brackets in the text refer to items in the bibliography.

Preface

The last two decades have produced immense changes in the world of language teaching, and nowhere have developments taken place more rapidly and more widely than in the teaching of English as a foreign language. The extent and nature of these developments is not always apparent in the most accessible form of publication, and this is hardly surprising. A great deal of the work is innovatory and experimental. It is subject to revision and may not find its way into more permanent publication until many years after it has been carried out. In any case, it is in the nature of TEFL that such work is very widely dispersed geographically, so that it is virtually impossible for the individual teacher or methodologist to keep in touch with all that is of potential interest.

The teaching of *English for Specific Purposes (ESP)* is an excellent illustration of the pace at which change may take place. While the training of students in specialized language skills has been carried out for many years, it is only in the last ten or fifteen years that professional attention has focused so clearly on the language needs of the specialist as opposed to the general language learner. Since the place of English as a foreign language in the curricula of educational and training institutions is increasingly justified in instrumental terms, the extent of teaching for specific and limited purposes is steadily growing. It has proved a dynamic field in the way it has stimulated innovation in approach and method on the part of the increasingly professional body of teachers engaged in such programmes. At the same time, it is in the nature of teaching for specific purposes that the solutions attempted, however innovatory and creative they may be, are applicable to the problems of the individual institutions or groups of learners and rarely become known outside the context for which they were first evolved. Of course, it must be supposed that sound general principles underlie such teaching, but the fact remains that much of what is new and exciting in ESP is known only to the few individuals who are directly involved, or to a handful of specialists with the time and opportunity to keep abreast of new developments.

Where fresh contributions to thinking about language teaching are being made simultaneously in so many parts of the world, where there is no clearly established body of previous research, practice or principle, where new ideas are often presented in relatively ephemeral form – conference papers, occasional papers, local journals, unpublished mimeographs – there is a need for a type of publication which will attempt to review and interpret the field so as to provide the wider dissemination of ideas among all kinds of EFL and other foreign language teachers that much of the continuing work deserves. At the same time, by attempting to provide near-exhaustive documentation of published materials and ephemera, such a publication will itself become a regular reference source for students and teachers wishing to familiarize themselves with developments at first-hand.

When Pergamon Press approached the Centre for Applied Language Studies and asked whether it would be willing to undertake just such a study of the field of English for specific purposes, we responded with great interest and enthusiasm. Believing that the Centre is well qualified to undertake such reviews, we welcomed the opportunity that such a commission would provide to assign one of our staff on a full-time basis to the task of documenting and assembling the relevant material and to carrying out an exhaustive analysis of the state of the art of ESP. We know that the exercise undertaken by Pauline Robinson will prove to have great value to the teaching of the Centre itself. We hope that the general EFL and foreign language teaching readership to whom the present publication is destined will also find that we have put in their hands an invaluable guide to the sometimes bewildering world of English for specific purposes.

D A WILKINS
Director,
Centre for Applied Language Studies,
University of Reading.

Introduction

English language teaching is notoriously subject to fashion, and one of the most prestigious fashions of recent years has been that of English for Specific Purposes: ESP. Although it has now been overtaken in topicality by other developments, notably self-directed learning, ESP is still the subject of much discussion and many key issues in ESP remain unresolved.

One of the important issues is the extent to which ESP is really different from general ELT. Many exciting new developments have occurred under the aegis of ESP, but all these ideas and techniques could equally well be applied in general ELT courses. The concepts of communicative competence, communicative language teaching, discourse analysis, and others, have all been associated with ESP, but what is represented here, in fact, is simultaneous but separate development, these various concepts stimulating development in ESP, yet not being contained by it.

The rapid rise to prominence of ESP has led to the publication of a large number of ESP textbooks. Any hope that a study of this wealth of material would answer the question, 'What is ESP?', however, would be frustrated, for the wealth of material is matched by the range of different approaches. A few books are obviously the product of careful research and of a clearly defined theoretical position. A number are general ELT courses in all but name. Too many of the published works represent an attempt to 'jump on to the bandwagon' of fashion, but others have developed from materials actually used on ESP courses in different parts of the world. Some of these courses have suffered in the attempt to make them more widely applicable; others have obviously gained by being well tested in real teaching situations.

The wealth of material available makes the task of an ESP course-leader who decides to choose a published textbook particularly difficult. The

British Council's English Teaching Information Centre (ETIC) Information Guide on ESP (45) is the most compendious bibliography on ESP to date and the British Council have been rightly congratulated on it by John Swales in his review (46). Swales nonetheless suggests a number of improvements, namely a critical review of the entries, more information about how to obtain items, reference to reviews of any of the items, description of major ESP projects, a section on teacher training and a section on journals. In addition one might request that very dated and/or unobtainable items be deleted from the Information Guide.

The present work represents an attempt to supplement, and in some areas expand, the British Council's Information Guide. The survey has been limited on the whole to works published within the last ten years, a high proportion of all British ESP publications being listed in the bibliography, many of them being discussed in the text. The survey cannot be complete, for new publications are appearing every week. The criterion for selection was that the work in question was described as an ESP book by the publisher.

In addition to books, a survey has been made of a large number of articles and documents, in journals and in manuscript form. Many important developments in ESP have never – or not yet – appeared in book form. Quintessential ESP, if we can pinpoint it, is perhaps this: materials produced for use once only by one group of students in one place at one time. With luck, samples of these materials and information about their genesis may be found in the British Council's ETIC archives. A few, very useful, publications have gathered together descriptions of particular ESP courses but much material still remains scattered, not readily accessible to the often hard-pressed teacher or course designer.

Much potentially useful material remains permanently inaccessible because it is classified information, that is material used on language teaching courses by the armed forces. A few articles describe elements of such courses, as taught in Britain, Canada and the USA but more information about materials and techniques would be valuable.

More information would also be welcome about courses run by commercial enterprises, since a preponderance of writing about ESP, especially theoretical writing, emanates from institutions within a state system of education.

The most prolific country in terms of ESP publications is undoubtedly Britain, but much exciting work is going on elsewhere, even though it does not always lead to publication. Important centres for ESP work are the Regional English Language Centre (RELC) in Singapore, the English Language Servicing Unit at the University at Khartoum (which produces *ESPMENA Bulletin*) and the University of Chile at Santiago. The parts of the globe represented by these centres: SE Asia, the Middle East, Latin America are all important 'consumers' of ESP and their special needs have stimulated much new development in ESP. ESP work of a slightly different kind has been in existence for longer in Europe, although it may not have been until comparatively recently that the term ESP was used to describe it. More recently we note that uses for ESP are being found in Canada and in the USA.

The concept of ESP is still fairly new, although its practices may have existed for some time. Definitions of ESP are numerous, the concept being fluid enough to support a number of interpretations. The present work cannot hope to be comprehensive but it is hoped that enough of the important influences on ESP, of the ideas associated with it and of the developments leading from it have been brought together to enable the interested teacher and student to have a clearer idea of what is involved in ESP and a more specific perception of its significance.

1. Definitions of ESP

'For the last ten years or so, the term "languages for special purposes" has begun to appear more and more frequently in language teaching literature.'

Thus wrote Ronald Mackay in 1976 (73). Ten years would seem to be a convenient span of time for looking back, for in Mackay and Mountford (59) the editors also refer to 'over the last ten years or so' as the period in which the concept of languages for special purposes became current. The first conference on languages for special purposes was convened in 1969 (64) which provides yet another starting point for consideration almost ten years later.

During our period of (rather roughly) ten years a wealth of terms has grown up. LSP (Language(s) for Special Purposes) is the international term and although most work on languages for special purposes has been on the English language, a consideration of some other LSP research provides a useful insight into some shortcomings and preoccupations of ESP.

The term ESP itself has changed its signification during our ten year period. Formerly standing for English for *Special* Purposes, the term now used by 'an increasing number of scholars, practitioners and institutions' is English for *Specific* Purposes [Munby (167)]. English for *Special* Purposes is thought to suggest special languages, ie restricted languages, which for many people is only a small part of ESP, whereas English for *Specific* Purposes focuses attention on the purpose of the learner and refers to the whole range of language resources. The abbreviation ESP will be used throughout this paper, and can be interpreted as representing either English for Special or Specific Purposes since the sources quoted can be seen to refer to the same entity, whichever term is employed.

In order to understand what is implied by ESP we can continue the quotation from Mackay (73):

> 'It (here ESP) is generally used to refer to the teaching/learning of a foreign language for a clearly utilitarian purpose of which there is no doubt.'

This utilitarian purpose is generally conceived of as successful performance in work, work in which the English language plays an auxiliary role. Thus by ESP is meant the 'teaching of English, not as an end in itself but as an essential means to a clearly identifiable goal.' [Mackay (163)]. Thus the *general* with which we are contrasting the *specific* of ESP is that of general, education-for-life, culture and literature orientated language course, in which language itself is the subject matter and the purpose of the course. The student of ESP, however, is learning English *en route* to the acquisition of some quite different body of knowledge or set of skills.

It is not easy, however, to characterize the 'clearly utilitarian' purposes for which students learn ESP. Perren (66) suggests in his foreword that *'language teaching for special purposes* is not very satisfactory as a blanket term to cover a variety of vocational and professional reasons for learning or teaching languages.' Mackay and Mountford (59) however suggest three kinds of purpose:
— occupational requirements, eg for international telephone operators, civil airline pilots, etc.
— vocational training programmes, eg for hotel and catering staff, technical trades, etc.
— academic or professional study, eg engineering, medicine, law, etc.

Strevens (81) modifies this when he suggests that 'All SP-LT (special-purpose language teaching) courses are either *occupational* or *educational* in nature.' He makes a further three-way distinction according to the timing of courses, and produces the following diagram: See Figure 1.

This three-way time distinction would seem to be a realistic one and Strevens' diagram is thus an improvement on that devised by the Ministry of Overseas Development (40) although the Ministry makes a further sub-division of EEP (English for Educational Purposes): See Figure 2.

Figure 1

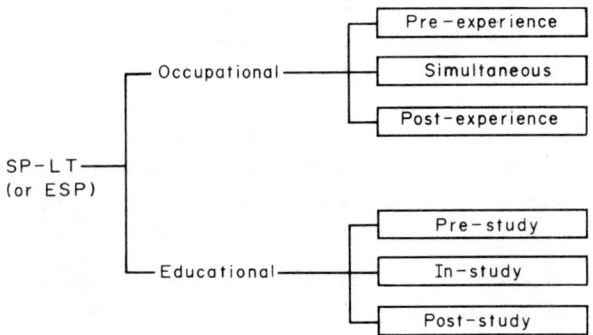

[*From Strevens (81)*]

Figure 2

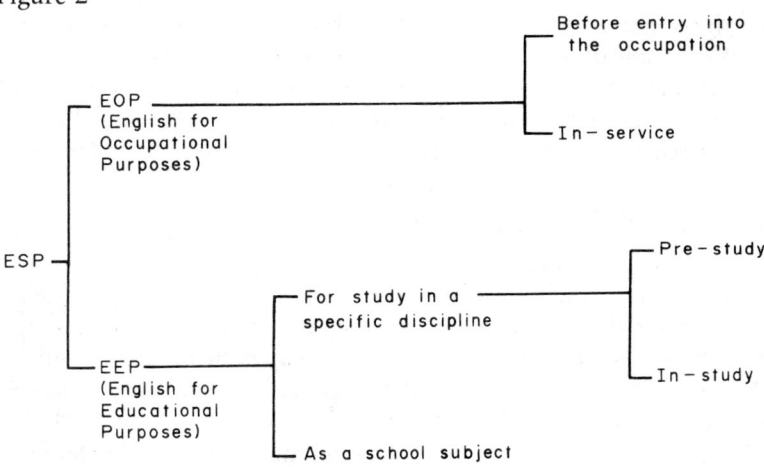

[*From ODM/BC (40)*]

It is not entirely clear what EEP as a school subject is, since this description could refer to the traditional type of general course against which ESP is reacting. Perhaps what is intended is EAP: English for Academic Purposes or study skills, ie how to study through the medium of English, regardless of the subject matter of the studies.

One more abbreviation must be introduced: EST: English for Science and Technology, which Mackay and Mountford (59) suggest is a major sub-division of ESP. Where would this fit in either of our diagrams? EST would seem to be both an occupational and an educational use of English: occupational when we are considering the needs of oil-field workers, engineers, computer programmers, etc; educational when we consider school and university students around the world studying Physics, Chemistry, Maths and Engineering through the medium of English.

At times it seems that EST, especially from the EEP point of view, is the most prestigious development in ESP. Mackay and Mountford's collection (59) is almost entirely concerned with EST and EAP; likewise most of the articles in the British Council collections (44), (47) and (48). One wonders if EST does not represent the attempt by English teachers around the world to show that they are intellectually capable of grasping the arcane wonders of science. It is, however, a healthy corrective to consider some of the work done in LSP in languages other than English lest considerations about EST dominate our understanding of ESP. (Although the largest number of ESP textbooks is in the general area of commerce, the largest number of articles refer to EST – see the bibliography and also British Council (45)).

We have seen that EST does not fit into either of the diagrams and this is because EST refers to subject matter rather than to activity: whether occupational (which includes Mackay and Mountford's 'vocational') or educational. This point leads on to another element in the definition of ESP, namely that it is the *purpose* for which the learner is studying that is *special* or *specific*, not the *language*. (This point is discussed further in Chapter 2.) A learner's purpose may be expressed as 'I want to learn English in order to be an international airline pilot' or 'in order to work in an oil-field in Saudi Arabia' or 'in order to study food technology at Reading University'.

The fact that the student of ESP can express his or her purpose succinctly suggests several other elements in the definition of ESP. The first of these is the time factor. As Fitzjohn says:

'The very concept for "special purposes" implies that foreign language study is a subsidiary contribution to another, main, interest, and that there will normally be pressure to achieve the required level of linguistic competence in the minimum of time.' (71)

Perren in his introduction (66) also refers to the pressure of time when he notes that 'In 1968 it was assumed that teaching a language to adults for special purposes often implied an intensive course. This still applies.' Certainly many teachers and designers of courses in the commercial and technical worlds refer to a time constraint (eg a three-week course for airline staff, described by Coutts (342) but the time factor is not mentioned by Munby (167) nor by Strevens (81) in their definitions. Those writing about ESP in tertiary education vary in the degree to which they acknowledge time constraints: most are referring to one-year courses, but a number refer to the necessity of selecting which skill(s) to teach when offered only a very few hours a week in which to teach.

Another element over which more people are agreed is that of the age of the ESP learner. For most people the learner is an adult or near adult. This seems obvious when we consider EOP: for people who are in jobs or about to take up employment. Even within EEP the dominance of EST has suggested that the learner is in tertiary education – in his or her own country or as a foreign student in Britain. However, there is evidence that in some parts of the world students are being prepared for university work or are learning science through the medium of English increasingly early in their school careers. As Michael Long writes in the editorial of the ESP section in *Edutec 3* (April 1975):

> The number of people wanting to learn English for a specific purpose is spiralling. By and large these people have been students in tertiary education, and adults. Increasingly, however, attention is being given to the possibility of equipping secondary age students for their anticipated language needs in higher education and future employment.'

One reason that the typical ESP learner was thought to be adult was the specific/general contrast. The typical general English course is that given at secondary school, starting with beginners and bringing them (it is hoped) to reasonable competence in all areas of the language. However, we must acknowledge that many adult education and evening classes are for language and culture, general language not ESP, so that the ESP cannot be considered the domain of adults exclusively or necessarily.

If the link of ESP with adults is made it is also sometimes assumed that the student of ESP is a post-beginner. That is, the student has done a general English course at school and now, as a young adult, wishes to extend or adapt this competence to his or her particular field of work or study. In those cases where the school course has been inadequate, the student actually needs remedial English, but, it is hoped, of a more purposeful kind than before. (See Bates (198) for example.) It is certainly true that in many cases an ESP course represents a re-direction in the study of English for an individual student – especially if the student is involved with EST at university level, but at the same time many students of ESP, especially in some commercial and technical fields, are complete beginners in the language.

The third element in a definition of ESP arising from the fact that the students of ESP can express his or her purpose in learning is this very purposefulness itself. Strevens (81) seems to express this in the first part of his three-part definition of ESP: '(1) In SP-LT the language-using purposes of the learner are paramount.' This implies two things: firstly that learner and teacher should be constantly aware of these purposes and not introduce irrelevant material into the course, and secondly, and more importantly, that an ESP course should be learner-centred. Munby (167) makes learner-centredness part of his definition, contrasting the goals of ESP courses with 'nonlearner-centred criteria such as the teacher's or institution's predetermined preference for General English or for treating English as part of a general education' (page 2).

Attention to the needs of the learner is certainly a key element in any definition of ESP; indeed for some, eg Munby, it is the crucial element. However, this does not mean that learner-centredness is unique to ESP: rather, the two concepts have developed side by side. Brumfit (70) asks whether new terms always mean new things and suggests that ESP is not necessarily a new approach but a new emphasis in teaching. Part of this new emphasis is on the learner rather than on the teacher or the education authorities, but courses which are learner-centred but yet not ESP are currently available on the market.

Implicit in the definition of ESP as purposeful learning and teaching is the idea that the purpose can be expressed and tested. Rather than studying for an open-ended period of time for a general examination, the student of ESP is usually studying in order to *perform* a *role*. The measure of success for students learning English for hotel waiters, or the English for food technology, is whether they can perform convincingly as hotel waiters in English or whether they can act appropriately as food technologists in English (and pass exams in food technology, rather than exams in English). This attention to successful performance in English rather than knowledge of the rules of English (or even the ability to write good general essays and *précis* in English) is part of a contemporary approach to ELT which again, like learner-centredness, while being particularly appropriate to ESP, is not peculiar to it. However, contemporary views of the importance of communicating or performing or interacting successfully in English are such that this ability is seen to be an essential element in the definition of any ESP course. Thus Brumfit (70) acknowledges that:

> 'First, it is clear that an ESP course is directly concerned with the purposes for which learners need English, purposes which are usually expressed in functional terms. ESP thus fits firmly within the general movement towards "communicative" teaching of the last decade or so.'

In the same way as the communicative movement has appeared innovatory and exciting in the last decade, so too has ESP, introducing what Strevens (81) calls 'fashion and the bandwagon effect'. He suggests that SP-LT shows signs of becoming fashionable. Courses are being labelled as 'special-purpose' language courses chiefly because that is what the course organizers believe will attract learners. Earlier in the same article, however, Strevens recognizes that it is difficult to draw the line between what is a special course and what is a general course. Even the archetypal general course, a school course, may be said to have a definite aim, namely to pass a certain examination. (It is the examination which is general more than the course.) Cannot books which aim to prepare students for one of the Cambridge exams, or which are aimed at tourists, or which contain a high proportion of commercial vocabulary or which concentrate on spoken English, say, or reading comprehension, be said to be specific? There are certainly ragged edges around any definition of ESP. Either this or the bandwagon effect encourages many publishers to offer some of their books (generally in the commercial field or language skill specific) as being suitable for ESP students even if not originally designed to be so.

At the other end of the scale one could say that the true ESP course will have only one student in it, since each individual student has different needs and purposes which an ESP course should aim to satisfy. This is perhaps why Perren in his foreword (66) objects to ESP as a 'blanket term' because it may suggest much similarity of problems or solutions where in fact there is very little... The paradox is that the making and publishing of courses presupposes identifiable *group* requirements rather than widely different individual needs.' There are indeed institutions where ESP is taught on a one-to-one basis [see Hughes and Knight (219)] but most of the materials we shall consider later (Chapter 2) were prepared for reasonably sized classes of students.

While not ruling out one-to-one classes, one might say that the usual ESP course is designed for a reasonable number of students with identical or nearly identical needs. The course is designed to satisfy those needs, which will be fairly specific and which will be occupation or study based. In addition the content of the course will be in some way limited. This Strevens makes the second of his criteria for defining ESP:

> '(2) The content of SP-LT courses are thereby determined, in some or all of the following ways: (i) *restriction*: only those "basic skills" (understanding speech, speaking, reading, writing) are included which are required by the learner's purposes; (ii) *selection*: only those items of vocabulary, patterns of grammar, functions of language, are included which are required by the learner's purposes; (iii) *themes and topics*: only those themes, topics, situations, universes of discourse, etc. are included which are required by the learner's purposes; (iv) *communicative needs*: only those communicative needs... are included which are required by the learner's purposes.' (81)

All of this may be summarized as limitation or, using one of Strevens' component terms, restriction. The most usual limitation when considering ESP materials is by subject matter, or theme and topic. Thus the British Council bibliography (45) subdivides according to subject discipline, eg Social Sciences followed by Physical Sciences, although one category – Study Skills – is determined by task or skill (Strevens' category of *restriction*).

We may summarize ESP courses as follows – modifying both Strevens' diagram and his text:

Figure 3

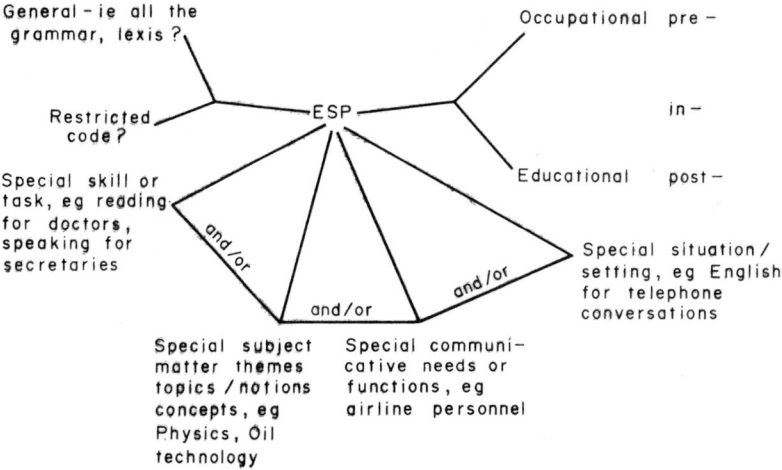

This diagram leaves open the question of special or restricted language. It also suggests that some elements may co-occur, most notably the element of skill or task with any of the others. Thus a course in reading comprehension must be aimed at a particular occupational or educational group, eg doctors and students of Medicine, or students of Physics, and not be designed merely for learners at X level.

In conclusion we may say that an ESP course is purposeful and is aimed at the successful performance of occupational or educational roles. It is based on a rigorous analysis of students' needs and should be 'tailor-made'. Any ESP course may differ from another in its selection of skills, topics, situations and functions and also language. It is likely to be of limited duration. Students are more often adults but not necessarily so, and may be at any level of competence in the language: beginner, post-beginner, intermediate, etc. Students may take part in their ESP course before embarking on their occupational or educational role, or they may combine their study of English with performance of their role, or they may already be competent in their occupation or discipline but may desire to perform their role in English as well as in their first language.

2. Survey of theoretical positions

In 1974 Perren (66) looked back over the past five years in ESP and noted that many questions still remained from the 1968 conference (64) and that many answers had still not been attended to. In many ways the situation is the same in 1978.

Some of the questions had perhaps been asked – and even answered – before 1968, since the origins of ESP are older than we generally recognize. In order to consider some of the theoretical issues now current in ESP it might be helpful to take a brief consideration of the history of ESP.

2.1 Historical survey of ESP

In his essay *English or Special English?* J D Corbluth (85) is healthily critical of the rise of ESP, urging teachers not to yield completely to the sway of a new ideology and to remember the general educational and cultural role of English. He suggests that special purpose teaching, in the sense of omitting items irrelevant to a particular group of students' needs, dates back to the work of Harold Palmer and Michael West.

Strevens (81) suggests that LSP has a much longer history than this, offering 1576 as the date of the first phrase book for foreign tourists. He decides however that 'Language courses of type "German for Science students" can more properly be regarded as the earliest form of SP-LT', without giving any dates.

Tickoo (87) and Lee Kok Cheong (86) both look at the development of ESP from the point of view of trends in linguistic analysis and in materials selection. Both suggest, without giving any dates, that the first stage in the development of ESP was eclectic and pre-linguistic; that is, not influenced by any particular theories of language or even of language teaching. Scientific English was looked at from the viewpoint of literature and seen to be needlessly complicated, not really different in kind, except perhaps in vocabulary, from ordinary language, but different in degree (of elegance).

However, Ewer and Latorre's *A course in basic scientific English* (322) was produced as the result of register analysis. Lee Kok Cheong divides register studies into two stages: firstly the analysis of the lexicon, considering in particular the frequency of occurrence of items and the presence or absence of items, and secondly the study of the syntax, as for example by Barber (89).

Tickoo suggests that subsequent to the study of register, there was an interest in skills-based materials (EAP, for example, presumably) but that not much was actually produced.

The most recent trend in ESP for Lee Kok Cheong is that of discourse analysis, which he sees as the most fruitful development so far. Probably Tickoo is referring to the same thing when he offers a cautious welcome to communicative-competence oriented materials, concluding with a recommendation for eclecticism in theories and materials.

2.2 Register analysis

Although methods of producing ESP materials based on register analysis are not the most recent, it is nonetheless relevant to consider what is involved in register analysis, since it is still a source of discussion and research. In 1977 Brumfit observes that 'ESP is also indebted to the tradition of analysis of functional style or register' (70) and the notion of register is obviously involved in any suggestion still made that English for *Special* Purposes must imply a special language. Particularly where a very short intensive course is concerned, where it is obvious that a drastic selection and reduction of language items must be made, the materials writer must be forced to employ notions of restricted language, or special language or register. However, as Perren writes in his introductory essay (66):

> 'There are, of course, considerable theoretical difficulties in attempting to isolate any "language of specialisms". The notion, for example, that a

distinctive "special" register (appropriate to a specialist subject) can be identified by contrast with a "general" register is fraught with confusion.'

Perren immediately exemplifies this confusion with a quotation from Halliday [in (64)] which suggests that while there is no such thing as a general register it is useful to recognize a category of 'special-purpose' languages or language varieties.

On the whole there is agreement that ESP does *not* mean a *restricted* language, although this is perhaps because most writing about ESP is concerned with students in tertiary education who will have experienced some years of a general English course and will therefore have a grounding albeit inadequate in 'common core' English. Coutts (342) was involved with short intensive courses for beginner-level airline personnel and obviously taught mainly a restricted code of fixed phrases. More might be written about strategies and techniques for such courses.

The problem for any textbook writer who wishes to base his material on register analysis is that research is either inadequate or non-existent. The most commonly quoted source of information on the language of science is Barber (89) but his data is really too limited for his conclusions to be usefully generalized. Other much-quoted research is that of Huddleston *et al*, although the report (104) is out of print and virtually unobtainable. Mackay and Mountford (350) write that 'we think that the Huddleston report is *not* of any great use to the language teacher. He seems to sidestep the principal question which is "How is the language of this field of activity different from the language of that field of activity?"' Swales (106) welcomes Huddleston (105) as the major source of statistical information but suggests that it is rather disappointing to the teacher of English, partly because it is confined to the level of the sentence.

Other research (eg Thakur (135) and Porter (115)) casts doubt on the existence of a clearly definable 'English of Science' finding many, often very different, sub-registers within science in English. The same point is made by Ewer and Latorre (202). They studied a corpus of over three million words, spread, as with the Huddleston study, over a range of 'brows', eg professional papers and monographs, advanced and undergraduate textbooks, specialized journalism, semi-popularizations. Among the 'surprises' to emerge from their study was 'the great variety within scientific English' such that different sub-registers had different structures. Any useful research, then, tends to confine itself to very limited, clearly defined, areas, for example prepositions in chemical abstracts [Sastri (119)], or noun adjuncts in an engineering text [Sears (121)] or Latinate names and article usage in biology [Swales (133)].

One must be careful, however, not to suggest that one feature, eg the type and sequencing of noun adjuncts, is unique to one type of text or that this one feature uniquely characterizes the text. As White (140) discovered:

> 'Firstly, it became clear that . . . it is not possible to take the occurrence of any specific feature as being criterial of one and only one particular register. Secondly, it was obvious that what made one register distinctive in comparison with another was a unique constellation of features rather than any single characteristic.'

White has sufficient confidence in the value of register studies to suggest that 'with sufficient data it would be possible to devise a series of register 'specifications', in which typical constellations of features could be specified for each register' (140). One must then ask what features, if not all, to study. Too often the term register is used to refer just to vocabulary and collocation. Garwood (100), in a very simplistic approach, seems to identify register with lexis and suggests a very elementary way of obtaining lists of lexical items, and later lists of structural items, in order to make up a syllabus. Anthony (88) gives a useful characterization of a lexical analysis, but, as many writers including Corbluth (85) have suggested, lexis, especially in EST, is probably more of a problem for the (arts trained) English teacher than for the student. Obviously more than lexis must be considered.

Chiu (95) analysed a large corpus of 'administrative English', both spoken and written, as used by civil servants, confining her attention to the choice of verb. As well as the choice of lexical verb, however, she considered the structure of the verb phrase. White (140) suggests a technique for quantifying data for the verb phrase, and also for the noun phrase, for types of adjunct, and for the sentence.

Although Chiu's corpus is fairly large (250,000 running words of administrative writing, 60,000 running words of 'topic-oriented boardroom discussions among high-ranking public servants') it would all seem to be material likely to be used by her students in their professional life. This contrasts with the work of eg Ewer and Latorre (202) who studied material eg monographs which their students (undergraduates) would probably not have to cope with. Friel (99), reporting on verb frequencies in legal English, and Kirkman (109), trying to find out how common 'common core' words are in certain Engineering and Maths texts, both conclude that ESP courses should be designed locally for specific target audiences with any register analysis confined to the particular set of textbooks for their special subject that a particular class employs. Thus Phillips *et al* (353), preparing a course for Agriculture students, made a study of four Agriculture textbooks, looking first at the verb phrase (lexical choice and structural choice), the sentence and the paragraph, and later at the noun phrase and adverbials.

This kind of work, namely undertaking 'statistical surveys of tense-frequencies, sentence-types, vocabulary, etc', suggests Swales (276) 'does provide a framework (in new EAP subject-areas) within which pedagogical selection can be made, even if the principles of such selection are only partly based on the frequency information'. Swales remarks, however, that 'such work is not now usually thought of as being of much direct use to course design' – but he does not elaborate on this.

One thing that is needed, as White (140) is advocating, is greater precision, and less generalization about the supposed characteristics of certain registers. Greater precision, or clearer specification of methods of selection, might prevent such conflicts as Corbluth (85) points out, for example that Swales, in *Writing scientific English* (334) suggests that main verbs in scientific texts are generally in the present simple tense whereas Close, in *The English we use for Science* (319) emphasizes the continuous form of the verb.

However, perhaps the study of the verb and/or noun phrase, even of sentence patterns, or sentence connection [as in Porter (115)] is not enough. Strevens (81), White (140) and Candlin *et al* (454) all suggest that an important consideration is purpose. White calls this 'the crucial determinant of language form'. Candlin uses the phrase 'communicative purpose', which suggests that the analyst is going beyond the study of words and the structures they are found in; certainly beyond the sentence, if not outside the text. Spencer (78) criticizes register studies for being confined to the text and suggests that what is important is role: when one is learning a new language (or a new variety of language) one is learning a new role. Spencer wonders whether one can teach an LSP without performing the accompanying role activity.

Widdowson (84) characterizes traditional register studies of lexis and structure as 'quantitative' and suggests that what is needed is a new 'qualitative' approach which would consider such things as communicative competence and role performance. He acknowledges that a methodology for such a qualitative approach has not yet been perfected, yet urges that studies be made and materials be produced. We may describe what he advocates as discourse analysis and the communicative approach.

2.3 Discourse analysis and the communicative approach

Discourse and discourse analysis have received much attention in recent years, but several different things are intended by the terms. *Discourse* may first of all refer primarily to spoken interaction, which will be analysed in terms of units of meaning, organized into a hierarchy employing some or all of the terms *act, move, exchange, transaction* and others. Secondly, *discourse* may refer to a stretch of language, either spoken or written, analysis of which will consider aspects of sentence connection, or cohesion. Widdowson [(153) and elsewhere] has suggested that it is more appropriate to use the term *text* here, not *discourse*, making the useful distinction between viewing a stretch of language as an exemplification of the structure of the language, especially of devices to indicate structuring above the level of the sentence (*text*), and viewing a stretch of language as a unique piece of communication (*discourse*). Incorporated in Widdowson's definition of *discourse* is the third generally used meaning of the term, which is employed to cover the consideration of *rhetorical functions* or *communicative purposes*.

The first meaning of *discourse*, where a spoken or a written text is analysed in terms of a hierarchy of constituent units, is best exemplified by Jones (147), although he later (182) almost dismisses this paper as 'a crude attempt'. A related study is made by Lilley (471), analysing a science lecture. Both Jones and Lilley make some suggestions for the preparation of teaching materials, but these do not seem to have been taken up, although other work, eg Moody (475), may be based on related ideas. Some of the work of Selinker, Trimble *et al* fits in here, most particularly Trimble (138) where the *physical paragraph* is distinguished from the *conceptual paragraph* (which may consist of several physical paragraphs). The conceptual paragraph is deemed to be the 'basic unit' of scientific and technical discourse and 'typical patternings' of rhetorical units are suggested within the conceptual paragraph. Like much of Trimble *et al*'s work this idea does not seem to have been utilized elsewhere, except for Drobnic (345).

The second meaning of *discourse* (or *text*, in Widdowson's terms) is exemplified when Halliday writes (in (66)) that 'special languages may be characterized by different distributions of grammatical patterns, special meanings of generally occurring patterns and by discourse features of connected text'. These features would include connectives (eg *firstly, moreover, such as*) and other devices of cohesion. Mackay (205) suggests that 'these markers (ie connectives) are particularly frequent and important in the tight, logically developed presentation of scientific information'. The use of connectives is one of the features which Porter (115) employs when differentiating kinds of scientific text.

Candlin and Murphy (338), reporting on a project to prepare lecture comprehension material for engineering students, review research into lecture comprehension and consider both *discourse*, in the first sense mentioned above, and cohesion. They note the importance of the study of discourse markers (indicators of transition between the stages of a lecture, between one act or one move, etc, and another) and of connectives – not because these are special to ESP but because the general ELT has so far ignored them. The study of cohesion, of discourse markers, etc would seem to be another trend in linguistics and language teaching which has developed alongside ESP and which is very useful to it but which is not uniquely contained by it.

The third meaning of *discourse analysis* relates to the study of rhetorical functions. These can be exemplified from Todd, Trimble and Trimble (358) referring to technical manuals:

> 'Thus we find commonly the rhetorical functions of description, definition and classification, and the rhetorical techniques of time order, space order and causality. In addition, manuals have two rhetorical features found less commonly in scientific and technical writing: the interpretation of illustrations and the rhetoric of instructions.'

Trimble and Trimble together with, variously, Selinker, Lackstrom and Vroman engage in the identification of the rhetorical functions in any given text or group of texts, consider the sequencing of functions, and analyse the forms of their linguistic realization, most particularly the verb forms. Their work on the relationship of tense and rhetorical function seems especially useful. Again, however, very little of this work has been developed, either elsewhere or at any length greater than the article. (One paper, Weissburg and Buker (305) makes use of the work by Lackstrom; and Hara (215) in Todd, Trimble, Trimble and Drobnic (69) is indebted to the Trimbles.)

Trimble and his colleagues have devoted their attention to EST – sometimes more to Science, sometimes more to Technology – but their discoveries would seem to be valid for academic English in general. Mackay and Mountford (350) hint at this when they write:

> 'Scientific language data... particularly lends itself to examination in such terms (ie of rhetorical functions) since the scientist is constantly involved in performing fairly explicit acts of defining, identifying, comparing, differentiating, classifying, etc.... I am not suggesting that the scientist is the only one who performs these acts – we all perform them in everyday life – but the scientist is more explicitly conscious of the procedure he is engaged in, he is much more conscious of the rhetorical value of the language he is using.'

Mackay and Mountford have not only written in a number of places about the theory and practice of ESP, but they have also produced materials, particularly Mountford, most notably volumes in the *English in Focus* Series (262). Along with Mackay and Mountford, then, we must consider the editors of the *Focus* Series, H G Widdowson and J P B Allen who have also produced detailed accounts of the nature of ESP.

The *English in Focus* textbooks exemplify an interest in connectives and in cohesion and also in the structuring (ie grammatical structuring) and sequencing of rhetorical functions. Like Trimble *et al*, Widdowson *et al* are mainly concerned with reading and writing, but Widdowson and his colleagues seem to have a more dynamic, a more obviously activity-based approach. Throughout, the words *communication* and *communicative* are used and there is a spill-over into the realm of spoken communication. As Mackay and Mountford put it (350): 'the *raison d'être* of the service language teaching department as we see it is to impart to the student the wherewithal to communicate adequately in a specific area' and later they justify the teaching of EST by suggesting that it facilitates 'the scientist or technologist in communicating adequately with his colleagues about his specialist field of studies in speech or writing'.

Allen writes (285): 'In preparing the *Focus* series we have consistently taken the view that an EST programme should aim to give effect to a communicative view of language' and Widdowson supports this (84) by stating that 'a concern with ESP/EST necessarily entails a concern with communicative competence'. We might ask, however, how this concern could manifest itself beyond the provision of exercise material in the devices of cohesion and in rhetorical functions. Widdowson (84) suggests that it is important that students feel that they are involved in a communicative activity and not just learning usage. Students need to be given problems to solve which 'should as far as possible make appeal to the kind of cognitive processes which it is the purpose of science teaching to develop'.

This last suggestion of Widdowson's is perhaps his most significant and controversial. It is significant because it holds a key to Widdowson's thinking and Widdowson, we must acknowledge, is one of the most influential thinkers in ESP. It is controversial because it makes a number of assumptions, not all of which can be justified.

Widdowson's first assumption concerns the universality of science. (The most important source for Widdowson's ideas here is (84), from which all following quotations are taken.) He writes:

'What I am suggesting, then, is that fields of enquiry in the Physical and

Applied Sciences, as these are generally understood, are defined by their communicative systems, which exist as a kind of cognitive deep structure independently of individual realizations in different languages.'

Widdowson assumes secondly that students already have some knowledge of science and some knowledge of English. 'These two must be put together.' Thus the English teacher will not be teaching language and rules of use as such (because the students already know them) but will be providing the students with an opportunity 'to induce meanings by reference to their own knowledge'. Equipped with a knowledge of science in his own language, a student will be seeking the mechanisms for the expression of that knowledge in English. Widdowson offers a definition of EST:

> 'EST is best considered not as a separate operation but as a development from, or an alternative realization of, what has already been learned of existing knowledge.'

Earlier in the same article Widdowson suggests that:

> 'We might say that EST is at one and the same time a variety of English, and a particular linguistic realization of a mode of communicating which is neutral with respect to different languages.'

The surface realization of scientific discourse in any language, eg English, will be a combination of verbal forms – unique to the language – and non-verbal devices, such as formulae and graphs, etc which are universal or 'neutral with respect to different languages'.

From this is developed Widdowson's most interesting practical suggestion, that of three-way translation.

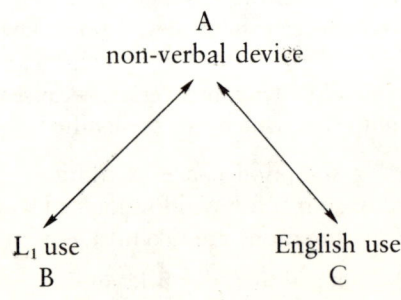

'The use of non-verbal devices enables us to relate three ways of expressing the same basic concepts and procedures.' The student can approach the formulation in English by means of both a non-verbal device and the formulation in his own language. The amount of support offered by the non-verbal device and by the student's own language can vary, and a range of interesting and practical exercises be produced: in which rather than learning rules the student is performing some of the activities of science.

Widdowson's ideas have certainly lead to a rethinking of methods and approaches and have led to the production of some interesting materials. But his basic assumptions must still be challenged and the limitations of his ideas acknowledged. In the first place Widdowson is writing about EST in tertiary education so we must not expect his ideas to be applicable generally in ESP or at lower academic levels. Even at the university level we can surely not assume as do Mackay and Mountford (350), probably following Widdowson, that 'students will have an advanced conceptual knowledge of objects, substances, processes and operations'. Many students at this level do not have much knowledge of science in their own languages because it does not exist in those languages. That is why they are learning science in English.

Within the area of skills, either language skills or study skills, many students lack the required competence in their L_1 (which is one reason for the development of EAP). Mackay and Mountford (222) suggest that reading comprehension is a universal skill which, like the concepts of science, can be transferred from one language to another. (So that the ESP teacher is concerned not with the skills as such but with the strategies for transfer.) But in a footnote Mackay and Mountford acknowledge that they are over-generalizing. 'In some cases in SE Asia and Central America, students' ability to read with comprehension in their mother tongue may be seriously limited.'

If we consider the timing of courses in ESP for students, then Widdowson's ideas are appropriate to post-experience courses. Attention is focused on the linguistic realization of what is already known, so that students are inevitably being taught language, although that too they are supposed already to know.

The majority of students of ESP, however, are probably pre-experience or in-service students, or are post-experience students with very limited or at least inadequate knowledge of English. Thus many of Widdowson's ideas will not apply to them, although use can certainly be made of his ideas for more dynamic methodologies and exercise types: in the interests of greater communicative competence being achieved and in the interests of student motivation.

2.4 Student motivation and the analysis of needs

> 'The adult learner on an intensive language course is highly conscious of himself and his purpose. The teaching programme is thus *learner-oriented*, and one must use economically what the adult learner brings to the class.' [Sculthorpe (190)]

Not all students of ESP are adults, but the majority are and, as we have noted above, ESP has developed alongside a new concern for the needs and feelings of the learner rather than the requirements of an externally imposed syllabus.

Views about student motivation and how it can be satisfied vary greatly, however. One of the important features of the *English in Focus* approach, suggests Allen (285), is that 'the student's interest is maintained because he can readily appreciate the relationship which is established between the English class and what goes on in the Engineering workshop or Physics lab'. But for many people the *Focus* approach has failed because the students are bored by dealing with what they know already. Although some teachers have suggested that the more academic Science students like to learn the intricacies of linguistic analysis, many are not interested in the manipulation of language items *per se*. However, if students are at times insulted by science (or other) material which they feel that they know already, they nonetheless demand relevance, although they may be satisfied with the lowest level of register variation, namely plenty of special vocabulary.

Macdonald and Sager (162) suggest that students would like to learn something new and propose that in universities 'foreign languages be taught jointly with academic subjects presented to a considerable extent in the foreign language'. This idea has been put into effect at the

University of Bath [Coveney (343)], in the Kingston–Cachan project [Root (354)], in Sweden [Davies (268)] and at a lower level in Singapore [Newberry (301)]. A few writers however, query what they see as an excessive demand for usefulness or relevance, characteristic of the communicative approach. Corbluth suggests (85) that many students have not in fact *chosen* their special subject and would like (or even need) their English lessons to introduce them to other ideas and subjects. Crofts (376) reviewing Jupp *et al, Industrial English* (375) complains that 'This is one of the standard features of ESP courses: they are so deadly serious, so earnestly work-oriented – so dull.' Davis (156) urges us not to forget general 'language-learning vitality' gained from such things as extra-curricular activities. O'Neill (169) also urges us to remember the element of fun and makes a more fundamental criticism of 'pure notional/functional syllabuses' when he suggests that it is impossible to predict everything that the learner will want to say. The learner should, presumably, then, be equipped with the generative power to say what is outside the syllabus.

Perren [(66) in the introduction] wisely points out that 'Identifying the learner's needs is a tricky business and we must beware of foisting on him needs which we think he should have but of which he is unaware.' James [in (66)] notes the problem of the variety of terms, for example *needs*, *demands* and also *wants*. McDonald and Sager (162) suggest that the identification of needs etc, depends on the level and experience of the student. If the student 'is already trained in his occupation his motivation is strong – he knows what he needs, and what he needs it for – and he can himself define the skills, purposes and language areas required. Learning a foreign language for him is a much simpler process ... than for the trainee (receptionist) who has not yet a clear conception of what he has to learn in his native language.' Even a trainee, however, can be encouraged to develop an awareness of his needs, according to the suggestions detailed by Richterich and Chancerel (172). Their document is a contribution to Council of Europe work on language learning by adults and places itself firmly within a learner-oriented systems approach. While the term LSP is not used, this is clearly what Richterich and Chancerel are concerned with. They suggest that the identification of a learner's needs is undertaken by three separate bodies: the learner himself, the teaching establishment, and the user-institution (ie the learner's employer). Information is sought regarding resources (the financial and technical resources of the learner and of the teaching establishment), objectives, methods of assessment, curricula, syllabuses and teaching methods (both ones preferred by the learner and the ones employed by the teaching establishment). The learner is encouraged to find out as much as possible about available language courses and to see how these match up against his resources, experience, objectives and inclinations.

Richterich and Chancerel suggest that needs analysis is an ongoing process and is certainly not confined to the beginning of a course. (Indeed they even suggest that it may not occur until after a course has begun.) They thus recognize that a learner's needs may change even while he is taking a language course, because of such diverse factors as a change in his financial resources, a change in his job, a modification of his objectives due to his (lack of) progress in the course.

When considering what use a learner may make of a language Richterich and Chancerel distinguish language activities (eg telephoning, writing letters), language functions (eg asking for information, arguing, explaining), language situations (eg face to face, in a working group) and the four language skills. They also list some of the different referential objects of language (eg everyday communication, scientific language).

The final part of Richterich and Chancerel's study is a comprehensive survey of all the different sources of information for a needs analysis. These range from surveys, questionnaires and interviews through language and intelligence tests to attitude scales to job and content analyses. Examples are given of each method and their relative values assessed.

Richterich and Chancerel's work is theoretical. Practical application of their approach is most evident in institutions concerned with self study. Survey of actual language use and of estimated needs are reported on by Lee (161) and James [in (66)]. Van Passel (170), Schroeder (173) and Gorosch (159) all demand more wide ranging research into needs and wants. Van Passel suggests that probably fewer people need to learn a language than we think and urges a 'much more accurate description of the most frequent language situations: a secretary taking down a report or message in shorthand, a delegate reporting on a draft proposal for a social reform programme'. He proposes the use of very detailed questionnaires for self-assessment of what students know of a language.

Of the methods suggested by Richterich and Chancerel the most commonly applied seems to be the questionnaire. Several people advocate the administration of a questionnaire at the beginning of a course in order to estimate students' needs and wants (eg Mackay (163)).

This is advocated as an essential (though necessarily last-minute) prerequisite to materials preparation by Webb (196), and Hughes and Knight (219). Allwright and Allwright (388) do not assume that it is easy to do a needs analysis: in fact a questionnaire may not discover all the needs, but the use of the questionnaire will demonstrate the teacher's interest in the students and lead to some useful discussion. The value of the teacher demonstrating his interest is stressed by several writers, eg Bates (198), referring to those adult students who are low on motivation because forced to do remedial English as part of their ESP programme. Teacher interest or 'pastoral care' is seen as an important component of the course. Drobnic (177) demonstrates the constraints on a needs analysis made prior to the start of a course. Books and other materials have generally to be ordered in advance of the arrival of the students. If the information on the needs and abilities of the students is inaccurate, then hasty adjustments have to be made − or students and teacher make do with inappropriate materials. On-the-spot needs analysis implies that the teaching institution possesses a very large bank of materials or that staff have methods for quickly creating them.

Apart from Richterich and Chancerel the most extensive theoretical study of the learner's needs is that of Munby (166), (167). Whereas Richterich and Chancerel pay comparatively little attention to the different dimensions of language use needed by a learner, language is Munby's primary concern. Munby's work represents 'a sociolinguistic model for defining the content of purpose-specific language programmes'. The model aims to give a valid specification of the target level communicative competence of a student and operates in two stages, firstly by building up a profile of student needs and secondly by converting these needs into syllabus content.

In order to 'construct a profile of the communication needs of a particular participant or category of participant' the model seeks information according to two sets of parameters. The first set of parameters concerns the type of ESP required and the particular educational or occupational purpose in question; the physical and psychosocial setting in which the language will be used; the social relationship in which the participant will be involved; and the medium, mode and channel of communication required. All these can be seen as primary, non-linguistic constraints on the language user. The second set of parameters concern linguistic data relating to dialect; target level required; the communicative event, ie *what* the participant has to do, either productively or receptively, which will involve consideration of topics and skills; and the communicative key, ie *how* the participant performs, which will involve consideration of attitudinal devices.

Having built up a profile of student needs, the next stage for Munby is to interpret the needs in terms of specific language skills and in terms of units of meaning together with the linguistic encoding for these units of meaning. From the language skills and linguistic encoding will derive the 'communicative competence specification' for the student or group of students in question. This is in effect a syllabus specification.

Munby's 'communication needs processor' is theoretical in that it lays out clearly and with great detail all the possible linguistic and socio-linguistic needs of a student on a language programme, but gives no indication as to how the data for an actual student might be collected. Participants on a British Council ESP Seminar (42) devoted to the study of Munby's work spent two days learning how to work with the communication needs processor, producing profiles of imaginary students. The seminar report (42) makes the surely surprising claim that 'There was no evidence that groups would have been better off using live informants.' Any real needs analysis is liable to suffer from a number of drawbacks, such as the lack of a common language between informant/student and teacher and lack of information regarding job specification either because the student is a novice or trainee in his special subject or because there is no access to the employee/subject specialist teacher, etc. Candlin *et al* describing the development of a study skills course (454) write that despite the fact that 'we set out to obtain as much information as we could.' 'We are perhaps in danger of producing a course for an audience which does not exist' – because adequate information was impossible to gather.

Despite the difficulties of information gathering, Munby's rigorous specification of the parameters of a sociolinguistic needs analysis and his useful taxonomies of social relationships and attitudinal tones make essential reading for the course planner. As Brumfit (168) writes: Munby's work is 'so detailed that many problems both practical and theoretical, can be examined far more clearly than had been possible in the past'.

2.5 Syllabus design

Munby's *Communicative syllabus design* (167) has been considered so far as a contribution to the study of needs analysis. For Munby, however, needs analysis is, as his title would suggest, the preliminary to the specification or design of a syllabus. Thus once a profile of a student's needs has been built up these must be realized in actual language forms, by means of the specification of language skills needed and the language functions. Munby gives an exhaustive list of micro-skills from which the shorter list of particular skills needed by a student can be assembled. Similarly Munby gives a detailed inventory of micro-functions, from which a selection can be made. Skills, functions and language forms together give syllabus content.

No one else has given such a rigorous and precise statement of one method of syllabus design as Munby. Although the systems approach to language teaching, which has developed separately but alongside ESP, suggests the sequence: needs analysis, syllabus design, methodology, implementation, evaluation, few people have attempted to work out a theoretical framework for any of the steps in the sequence. Jones and Roe (182) present a speculative approach to the analysis of needs, ends and means, which can be interpreted as an approach to syllabus specification (some more practical statements are made with reference to a syllabus for an academic reading programme), but their work serves mainly to highlight problems and shortfalls of knowledge and theory.

Swales (231), discussing teacher training for ESP, suggests that there is 'a new and general upsurge of interest in syllabus design' but this only appears evident at a practical, even *ad hoc* level, not in terms of theory. As so often in ELT and, more particularly, in ESP, it seems that linguistic and applied linguistic theory lags behind applied linguistic/language teaching and learning practice. Thus Mackay and Mountford (59) and British Council (48) present useful case histories of various ESP courses, but these are often anecdotally presented and the designer's concept of a syllabus has to be assembled piecemeal by the reader.

Hirayama-Grant and Sedgwick (180) present a well organized account of syllabus design, but their conclusions are worth repeating, almost in full:

> 'This paper has set out, with as much clarity and honesty as possible, the *a priori* and *ad hoc* sequences of decisions and procedures involved in the preparation of an ESP syllabus. It has been an extremely difficult but enlightening experience to specify the directions and meanderings we followed in arriving at an acceptable functional syllabus for teaching the restricted repertoire of air traffic control . . . Through placing our syllabus design project in retrospect, we have become aware of the great importance of intuitive factors in design work . . . in reality *ad hoc* decision-making, intuitive and educated guesses provided much of our momentum and direction. Because of their strong influence, these factors merit more attention in the literature of ESP.'

One essential feature of an ESP course is selection of material, provoked by shortage or pressure of time. Thus a feature of an ESP syllabus will be the absence of certain items found in a general course, or a focus of attention on certain things. The focus of attention may be determined by skill, by function, by topic, by situation, etc. (We may note that for Munby all syllabuses will comprise skills and functions, although the priority in their relative order of specification may alternate depending on the learner's needs.)

The selection of subject matter or topics is often 'given', although Webb

Survey of theoretical positions   33

(196), acknowledging the 'face validity' of labels, eg 'Medical English', warns us not to make the definition too narrow so that one is 'obscuring similarities across subjects' nor too wide to be really relevant.

Although the selection – and even more the ordering – of functions and settings is by no means uncontroversial, more has been written about the selection of skills, perhaps because the study and possible selection of skills has been acknowledged as an element of course design for much longer than that of functions.

For many people the traditional fourfold analysis of skills is sufficient, and it is suggested that a course may be built around just one of these skills.

Smithies (193) suggests that the EST student only needs reading, writing being much less needed by students than is often thought. Swales (304) also identified reading as being his students' greatest need but elected to prepare materials on writing since he felt that this was where he could be of more help. Some of the surveys of language use however suggest that skills are usefully – or naturally – combined. Thus the SCHML Report (41) assumes that course objectives will be low, for example a reading knowledge only, but nevertheless suggests that the teaching of pronunciation will help the development of reading ability – and also contribute to motivation. The same point is made by Corbluth (85). Candlin and Murphy (338) suggest that 'the teaching of fluent reading could be facilitated by combining it with a programme of training in listening comprehension'. Lee (161) found that 'The language activities of businessmen do not however slot neatly into the conventional four areas of language skill . . . since they often demanded a mixture of skills.' (Almost half – 49% – of the people responding to Lee's questionnaire listed 'listening and speaking', combined, as their greatest need.)

It is primarily in the area of EAP, it seems, that syllabus designers have acknowledged, as does Munby, that the traditional four skills division is no longer appropriate. Thus listening to lectures (which could be termed an *activity*) involves both listening and writing (specifically note-taking, which might be considered a *micro-skill*) and perhaps speaking as well. McDonough (472) suggests that rather than grading the language items in a listening comprehension course, the components of the skill should be graded (eg progressing from intensive to global listening).

Candlin *et al* (453), (454) distinguish between macro-skills and micro-skills, although it is not at all clear what is meant by each label. *Reading* appears to be described as a macro-skill, but so does *reading comprehension* and *listening comprehension*. *Reading* is additionally termed an 'epiphenomenon'. A series of macro-skills is related to a list of study modes: for example, under the mode of lecture we find listening comprehension, note-taking (surely a lesser activity than listening comprehension?) and 'ordering points in a hierarchy of importance'. It later appears, however, that these three lecture-related skills are perhaps the micro-skills into which each 'macro-skill was further analysed (notionally)' in order to allow 'us to plan the activities of our course and select appropriate linguistic data'.

Whatever the focus of a syllabus its implementation is likely to be constrained by such factors as the supply of teachers and funds, by local patterns of culture, even by political factors. Consideration of these factors is deliberately omitted by Munby, but is considered in some of the accounts of particular courses and syllabuses [eg Bates (198)]

2.6 Materials production

Once a syllabus has been specified (or, very often, while it is being specified) the ESP course director has to begin the task of materials production. After all, one of the obvious differences between ESP and general ELT is that the ESP teacher will not expect to use a general coursebook organized around general human interest topics, situations, functions, etc but will expect at least that the topics and situations that the language is linked to will relate to the students' subject specialism. Despite the growing number of published ESP textbooks, a great many subject specialisms are still not catered for, and even textbooks which are appropriate in terms of subject matter, may be inappropriate in terms of level, of function and of skill. It thus seems to be an unavoidable facet of the ESP teacher/course director that he should be materials writer as well.

As with syllabus design, much helpful information for the intending materials writer can be gleaned from the various published case studies, even though reference is not usually made to any sort of theoretical framework for materials production and though each case is very different. Some sort of systematization of the various approaches would be welcome.

For many people the starting point for materials production is the gathering of authentic data since the use of authentic data is seen as an essential component of any ESP course and also of any communicative syllabus, the communicative approach having developed alongside ESP. The term *authentic data*, however, is often used with a basic ambiguity so it is perhaps better to employ an earlier word, namely *realia*.

Thus Coutts (342) placed her tape-recorder on the desks of airline personnel before drawing up her list of utterances to teach. Sculthorp (190) describes visits to factories in Germany and England 'collecting samples of recorded speech in selected environments', and Davies (268) describes similar visits to Germany by a group consisting of both language and business studies teachers.

For more academic courses, materials writers seek printed realia, perhaps 'a coarse study of a large amount of material' [Ewer and Latorre (202)] or simply a very small number of textbooks likely to be read by (or actually prescribed for) a particular group of students [Phillips *et al* (353)]. (See also 2.2 above.)

Once a collection of realia has been made, however, opinions differ as to how it should be utilized. Sculthorp (190), for example, notes that 'This is not to say that authentic tape recordings can necessarily be used in their raw state, even though students appreciate the relevance of such materials.' Some listening comprehension courses, however, are based on long stretches of unadulterated authentic speech.

Differences of opinion harden when we consider the origin of reading passages in textbooks. Much objection has been levelled in recent years against reading texts which have obviously been composed by the language textbook writer for the purposes of exemplifying selected structural and lexical items. The objection is that since the passages do not derive from the 'real' world outside the language teaching classroom or the textbook writer's study, they will not help (or will even hinder) the student who wishes to use language in the real world. It is suggested that real passages be used so that the student will rehearse the steps he will perform in real life [see in particular Phillips and Shettlesworth (208)].

It is possible, however, that those who advocate the use of authentic – ie real – data are confusing *authenticity* with *relevance*. Relevance is generally desired in a course, but it is possible to have realia which is nonetheless not exploited interestingly or usefully or which is simply not relevant to a particular class of students. Conversely much relevant and interesting material has been used on many courses without being authentic.

Morrow (207) cautions us against the 'blind use of authentic texts' – because they are more particular and individual than we realize. He suggests that every text has a 'topic, function, channel and audience' – which are particular to it. Each of these must be matched with our target situation. Too often texts are selected on the grounds of topic only, so that while being authentic they are not relevant, at least on the grounds of function, channel and audience.

A more serious objection to the use of authentic texts is made by Widdowson (212) when he suggests that we are misusing the term *authentic*. He writes:

> 'I am not sure that it is meaningful to talk about authentic language as such at all. I think it is probably better to consider authenticity not as a quality residing in instances of language but as a quality which is bestowed upon them, created by the response of the receiver. Authenticity in this view is a function of the interaction between the reader/hearer and . . . the writer/speaker. We do not recognize authenticity as something there waiting to be noticed, we realize it in the act of interpretation.'

Thus to present a student on a language course with a sample of the language use he is expected to cope with at the *end* of his course, and to expect him to grapple with it (as seems to be advocated by many proponents of the use of authentic materials) is to misuse authenticity. If the student cannot fully understand the language he is exposed to, if communication fails because of the student's imperfect knowledge of the language, then, according to Widdowson, the language in question is not authentic at all.

Widdowson thus advocates the construction by materials writers of reading texts which are within the competence of the students concerned. Paradoxically these constructed texts are more truly authentic than anything from the 'real world' because only the constructed texts will achieve true communication with the students. In this way Widdowson justifies the type of constructed text which appears in the *English in Focus* series, which represents a distillation of the typical features of writings in the subject area in question, without the potentially distracting idiosyncracies of individual writers. Widdowson's justification is persuasive, but the problem still often remains of how to bridge the gap between such constructed texts – even if graded in terms of difficulty – and the frequently untypical, idiosyncratic texts of the real world. Jumping in at the deep end is not the answer, but neither is the wearing of water wings for ever.

Phillips and Shettlesworth (208), however, suggest that the preparation of specialized materials (eg the construction of appropriate reading texts) 'to a higher standard' is not practicable 'when one is dealing with a diversified demand often on a 'one-off' basis at very short notice'. They offer two modes of utilization of authentic materials. The materials can be graded in terms of *accessibility*, taking into account 'the absolute length of the passage, the density of new information and the presence of supportive graphic features'. Alternatively, the grading can be applied to the tasks which are undertaken, using the authentic materials as stimuli.

Phillips and Shettlesworth's point about the practicability of certain types of materials production has been taken up by Abbot (197) in a short and critical article on some of the 'fundamental problems in ESP'. He notes how exhausting it is to have to write materials while at the same time being expected to teach and run a course and wonders whether 'a valid model for the provision of specific purpose English' cannot be constructed which will allow 'more generally applicable materials' to be used.

2.7 Methodology

> 'Contrary to a surprisingly common misapprehension ESP does not rely for its successful implementation on some new and magic system of classroom methodology but on all the methods evolved over the decades by 'conventional' ELT: methods, in fact, are far less important than appropriateness of linguistic content.'

Thus writes Ewer (26). Others agree with him, for example, Webb (196) and Gorosch (159).

Some writers, indeed, take pains to demonstrate that familiar equipment or methods which might be thought inappropriate for ESP can in fact be used for it, for example simple audio-visual aids [Hilton (218)], and the language laboratory [Swales (226) and Lee (220)]. Swales describes some lively and interesting language lab drills for use on a service course, such as a sequence of listen to instructions – draw a diagram following the instructions – write a paragraph describing the diagram. The exercises could equally well be used on a general language course. Lee describes a language laboratory course to teach a reading knowledge of French to first year undergraduates. Such a use of the language laboratory seems fairly well established in British universities, judging by articles in (66) and elsewhere. Lee's approach is perhaps new in that students approach the target text by means of a preparatory one which presents the main ideas in a simplified way. 'Too often the language (lists of vocabulary and structures, presumably) is given before the ideas.'

Despite what Ewer believes (above) there seems to be a general feeling that the methodology of ESP instruction both in the classroom and in the textbook should be somewhat different from what has gone before. Hesketh (217) stresses the need for a teacher who is flexible and adaptable, and Drobnic (177) similarly emphasizes the importance of flexibility in an ESP course, especially regarding books and materials. Even Ewer in the same report (26) remarks that 'ESP is a system in its own right, and is not simply 'something extra' which can be tagged on to the body of conventional practices and assumptions subsumed in "general" ELT.' He stresses the value of a modular course, not relying on one textbook alone, but using a variety of materials.

Other possible features of an ESP methodology derive from its association with communicative and functional approaches to language teaching. Thus Webb (196), while suggesting that teaching methods for ESP are not different from those of ELT, at the same time refers to new or different uses of games, projects and role play. Fox (203) bemoans the absence of materials and exercise types for 'the new functional approach'. Allen (285) also requests new exercise types but rather confusingly wants them to be used 'across the whole spectrum, elementary and advanced, around the world'. Crofts (28) reports that participants at an ESP conference would have liked more practical suggestions on what to do.

It is probable that some of the exercise types associated with ESP are in fact entirely appropriate to general ELT but have arisen with ESP because of its greater attention to relevant language practice, to students' motivation and needs, and to efficiency of teaching and learning. Thus in particular the use of diagrams, both in textbooks and as classroom tools, although we must note that imaginative use of diagrams is very often associated with technology, where a diagram would usually be a teaching point in itself as well as a means of presenting a linguistic point. (See Beardwood *et al* (362), Hara (215) and Bartolic (336) but also Mead and Lilley (272) referring to Economics.) While considering ESP textbooks, however, we must note that many of them present the specialist material in a boring and/or traditional way, with either a minimum of exercises or a plethora of textbook-bound practice material. New types of subject matter need not produce new methods of exploiting it.

One of the newer types of methodology with which ESP is associated is that involved in the use of authentic materials. Authentic texts have been discussed above (2.6) but we might consider the place of authentic activities. The second Isfahan conference on ESP (27) suggested that 'Methodology ... must at some stage involve stimulation, role rehearsal, approximation of real-life language usage and a concern with authentic information.'

If the goal of an ESP course is for students to be able to perform certain real life operations, eg conduct a scientific experiment, mend a water-

pump, audit some accounts, etc then it can be argued that students should perform some or part of these operations while on the language course. Thus we find courses where some or all of the teaching is done in a laboratory or workshop [eg Jones (348)]. For Phillips and Shettlesworth ESP and the use of authentic materials seem to be inextricably linked but they characterize (185) 'the course-writer's Scylla and Charybdis as:
(1) The possibility that theoretically valid (authentic?) materials are distorted in practice by the nature of the classroom.
(2) The complementary danger that the materials are written for the classroom and the target ("real performance") neglected.'

Elsewhere (186) they suggest that the classroom situation leads to 'the illustrative use' of language, ie language about language and although teachers assume that students will effect the transfer to using language to express real needs and transactions, this does not in fact happen. Phillips and Shettlesworth urge a 'more flexible approach' aimed at replicating target type discourse with a minimum of pedagogic discourse. For this, presumably, they would reiterate their suggestion in (185) that authentic materials (presumably artefacts) be imported into the classroom and authentic operations performed on them.

An opposing view is taken by Widdowson (212) (see 2.6 above) who attacks the direct confrontation of students with authentic texts on the grounds that this confuses terminal or target behaviour with the means to obtain it. He writes that 'The pedagogy of any subject aims at guiding learners towards their terminal behaviour by the contrivance of appropriate intervening stages.'

The problem is ascertaining what these intervening stages should consist of. Fruitful lines of research lead into the components of the skills involved and ways in which these may be practised, but not enough has been discovered as yet.

2.8 Generalizability of materials

What has been ascribed so far to ESP suggests that each course must be different, each uniquely geared to the purposes, interests, etc of the students taking part in it. Certainly advocates of rigorous needs analysis would say so, as for example Allwright and Allwright (388): 'ESP teachers, in particular, should be conscious of the dangers of generalizing from one learning/teaching situation to another.' Currie *et al* (390) referring to a somewhat similar course write that 'there are no blanket applications of the technique', although at the same time they consider the possibility of it being suitable for some engineers and scientists. Crofts (376) identifies 'an inherent disadvantage of any course based too narrowly on functional criteria: it is not readily applicable or adaptable to situations differing significantly in functional features'.

The very method of constructing an ESP course may prevent the re-use of any of the material, for courses may be designed around the particular special subject textbook of one class of students or result from a full survey of on-the-job requirements' of a more technical group, resulting in a 'tailor-made course' [Gerighty (178)]. Opitz (183) criticizes the producers of *English 900* for imagining that the same material could be appropriate the world over, but nonetheless there is a world-wide demand for series such as *Nucleus* (265). Perhaps this is because of the common feature of ESP courses: shortage of time for preparation (and for teaching). Certainly there are few institutions like SLC (Specialist Language Courses) in York, England [as reported in Hughes and Knight (219)], which cater for the class of one, or analysts as painstaking as the Trimbles, whose materials are sometimes prepared for one individual student.

3. Analysis of current publications

3.1 Survey of what is available

A study of the British Council Information Guide on ESP (45) will show that by far the largest number of ESP textbooks is in the area of commerce (101 publications). Many of these are rather out-of-date and some are out-of-print or at least difficult to obtain. It is probable that the production of textbooks for commerce has the longest history within ESP, as the other early forms are rather marginal (language for tourists) or concerned with teaching rather than textbook production (reading knowledge of language for scientists). The English of commerce is also the largest non-academic type of ESP. On the whole, non-academic materials and non-academic teaching are under-represented in the published materials. One would expect more non-academic technological material to be available than actually is.

Technology, however, accounts for the next largest group of publications listed by the British Council (78 textbooks divided into groups of 'General', 'Engineering', 'Transport' and 'Agriculture'). After this we note Physical Science (46 publications), the Social Sciences (28 publications) and Medicine (23 publications). The British Council list is not quite complete, but it is by far the largest and most useful guide for ESP textbooks and articles and is thus a useful reference source.

If we consider articles describing the writing of textbooks or discussing the preparation of materials not intended for publication we note that there is virtually nothing in the area of commerce. Nor is there a great deal on the Social Sciences. Most articles on preparation and on methodology are in the academic area and concern EST (which can also embrace Medicine). Those teachers and course-designers in the non-academic areas who do write about their work stress the pressure of time on what are usually intensive courses. As their work involves a number of interesting differences from academic EST (a higher proportion of beginners, for example) it would be useful if more were written about what they do.

3.2 Summary of the main features of the available textbooks

The textbooks studied represent the full spectrum of views on language and language teaching. It is perhaps noteworthy that there seems to be no connection between modernity of method and approach, and popularity and apparent commercial viability. A number of writers and publishers claim to have adopted a 'communicative approach' but rather fewer in practice actually have.

Among the most interesting developments are the *English in Focus* series, and *Nucleus*, about both of which a great deal has been written, especially the former. *English in Focus* seems to be the only series produced as a result of extensive theoretical preparation and results can be compared with the expression of that theory. Also of interest are the various materials produced by ELTDU (English Language Teaching Development Unit) and Oxford University Press, and although these are clearly the products of a well-prepared approach to course and materials design, nothing has been directly written about this approach.

Very few textbooks are based on any kind of register analysis, although a number of books in the area of science make reference to the supposed importance of the passive. Some course-writers refer, however, to the value of collecting samples of language used by people in different work situations and using that language or work based on it for their courses. Many reading courses use authentic texts. This authentic data is selected on the basis of the user's intuition about its suitability and typicalness, however, and may not be typical of a register according to statistical analysis of features.

Most textbooks have been prepared for adults, although some of the newer ones [eg *Basic English for Science* (321)] are for use in schools. Most books assume an intermediate level of competence, but a great many, including those aimed higher, include some general, even remedial grammar practices as well as work on the 'special' grammar of the subject area.

One of the boasts of ESP courses is that they produce a high level of motivation in students because they are 'relevant'. Certainly a number of textbooks appeal through their generous use of authentic-looking diagrams, reproductions of documents and good photographs, although a correspondingly high number disappoint because of their lack of diagrams or use of poor quality photographs and 'artistic' rather than 'real' drawings. Some textbooks with an obviously relevant content nonetheless fail to maintain motivation because the format of each unit is tediously identical, whereas some conventionally-conceived and not always theoretically-relevant works maintain interest through lively exploitation techniques.

A few textbooks listed in the British Council Information Guide (45) have been produced outside Britain (generally elsewhere in Europe) and a few have been designed for particular linguistic groups. Both these sets of books seem to concentrate more on vocabulary and translation rather than anything else. Although some other textbooks have been conceived in particular (usually foreign) teaching institutions, in their published form they now aim to appeal to a world-wide market, sometimes at the expense of a dilution of concentration and relevance, particularly in the selection of skills and topics.

Grading of material – if at all apparent – is most frequently by grammar, although in some reading courses it is by length of text (not always with accompanying complexity).

Most textbooks are defined by topic, and as this is how the British Council organizes its bibliography/Information Guide, this is how a number of the textbooks currently available will be discussed here, but beginning with a consideration of several series of books.

3.3 Series of books

3.3/1 English for Careers Series (261) Regent's Publishing Co Inc, New York.

Each book in this large series aims to give an introduction to the specialized language of a different professional and vocational field, for example, tourism, computer programming, hospital services, air travel, etc. The books are not training manuals but, as the introduction to each book in the series states, aim to give 'a general introduction to both the opportunities and the problems involved' in each field covered. The students are assumed to 'be acquainted with most of the structural patterns of English. . . . His or her principal goals as a learner should be to master vocabulary, to use the various structural patterns in a normal mixture, and to improve his or her overall ability to communicate in English.'

There is thus no suggestion that any of the fields covered require any special structures. The emphasis is exclusively on vocabulary. 'Special terms' are introduced and explained at the beginning of each unit, often in fairly difficult language. Then follows 'vocabulary practice' consisting of questions on the vocabulary list, which can usually be answered simply by repeating the vocabulary list. Next comes a somewhat long, pedestrian and repetitive text, which utilizes all the new vocabulary. After this a 'Discussion' section tests comprehension but only requires repetition from the text. Finally the 'Review' practises the vocabulary with slot-filling exercises. Some of the books in the series have more interesting exercises related to diagrams, but these are still language practice exercises, not imitative of the real life activities of the profession concerned.

It is not clear how students are to 'improve' their 'overall ability to communicate' as no skills are referred to and there is no teacher's book. The vocabulary is quite difficult (and, despite disclaimers, rather American) and one wonders if the teacher would not need to know something of the specialist subject concerned.

3.3/2 *English in Focus Series* (262) Oxford University Press.

The *English in Focus* books were much heralded and in consequence, perhaps, have been much criticized for failing to live up to the high expectations. The books aim 'to develop in students who are entering higher education an ability to handle the kind of written English that they will be concerned with as an integral part of their specialist subjects . . . The purpose is to make students aware of the way English is used in written communication, and thereby to help them develop techniques of reading and to provide them with a guide for their own writing.'

The books certainly help with reading, but the writing practice is over-controlled and at times is closer to comprehension and grammar practice. If students can cope with the reading passages and some of the exercises on them, it should be assumed that they can cope with much freer and lengthier writing passages. Despite their clearly defined aim the books are accompanied by taped readings of the texts and of the answers to some exercises – supposedly to help with pronunciation, though this could surely have been equally well printed in the books in transcription.

Each book in the series follows the same format (with a few variations in labelling). Each of the eight units (except in *English in Biological Science*) begins with a reading passage 'within which are inserted sets of comprehension checks in the form of statements which may or may not be correct'. Thus the learner is encouraged to think as he reads. Solutions are provided at the end of the passage and wrong as well as right answers are discussed. This seems a good idea (as is the numbering of each sentence in the text for easy reference) but in practice, apparently, students too often find the explanations obvious and become irritated with a technique which is repeated right to the end of the book [see (312) and (403)].

One of the virtues, however, of the *English in Focus* books is that they contain plenty of exercises, so that students are forced to be active in their use of language, although some of the exercises are too mechanical and others are insufficiently explained. The trio of exercises immediately follow the reading passage *focus* on aspects of it as a *text*, this being one of the main elements in the rationale of the course (see articles by Widdowson, Allen, Mackay and Mountford referred to in Section 2.3 above). One exercise involves contextual reference. This students apparently find easy to do – in the classroom – yet cannot generalize from it to help them with other reading. 'Rephrasing' – searching in the text for synonyms for words in the exercise – is generally thought useful both for vocabulary consolidation and as search reading practice. 'Relationships between statements', however, which practises the use of connectives, eg *however*, *therefore*, is found by users to be insufficiently guided and explained. The material is important but students find it difficult, partly because it is new to them, and thus requires much more contextualized practice than is provided. The exercises certainly involve the students in 'going back and back into the text' as intended although the reading passages are 'unfortunately short and have been worked to the bones' (371).

Of the remaining exercises, some focus on grammar, supposedly those points 'which have a high frequency of occurrence and, more importantly, clearly identifiable use in scientific writing' [Allen (285)]. Thus we find the familiar structures of most books in scientific English, for example short form relative clauses, noun+noun constructions, -ing structures, and the passive. Given that the *English in Focus* books emphasize 'communicative relevance', the problem is how to apportion the grammatical material throughout each book so that it relates to the reading passages. Too often this is not achieved. A further disappointment is that many of the grammar exercises are traditional mechanical rewriting exercises, eg joining two sentences with a relative pronoun or joining groups of phrases between bar lines. Moreover, although all the material is about mechanical engineering or whatever, the sentences in an exercise may not relate to each other [see (371)].

A similar problem of relating exercise material to what is in the text occurs with the functions that are taught, eg defining, classifying, etc. Castanos (288) criticizes this 'de-contextualization' of function suggesting that it may either change meanings or at least inhibit students' comprehension.

Not all of the exercises in *English in Focus* fail, however. Much praise has been given to the 'Information transfer' exercises, involving writing from a diagram, or producing a diagram to explain a text. A great range of interesting and authentic-seeming diagrams, charts, etc are used and the chief complaint is that they are not used even more. For example, the 'Guided writing' at the end of each unit is criticized by Swales and Fanning (403) for being too mechanical (with the 'correct' version too close to the exercise). They suggest that it could be linked to note-taking strategies, for example, which might also involve diagramming. This in fact has been done in *English in Social Studies* and in *English in Biological Science*, both published in 1978, and both of which contain a number of improvements, especially in terms of study skills techniques and lengthier explanations, on their predecessors.

No textbook can be perfect for any particular class, and this is especially a problem for ESP. Some of the criticisms of *English in Focus* derive from its being used at the wrong level. There is no grading in any of the books in that each unit is the same in complexity and in task. Nonetheless within each unit there is great variation in the difficulty level of the tasks, some requiring more explanation than is given. Users of the book find that students generally like to learn new information and are thus a little impatient, if, as the authors intend, the scientific content is within their competence. The general conclusion seems to be that *English in Focus* is 'theoretically sound but pedagogically weak' [Tay (312)].

As Lee Kok Cheong concludes:

> '*English in Mechanical Engineering* is pioneering work however and has succeeded in injecting a breath of freshness to the study of English.' (371)

And Knight writes that

> 'Again, whatever reservations there may be about overall approach, the book (here *English in workshop practice*) nevertheless contains various exercises which would be a joy to work with, both as elegant solutions to language learning problems and as harmonic (*sic*) combinations of realia from the typical workshop textbook and language practice.' (380)

3.3/3 English for Special Purposes Series (263) Evans Brothers.

This is a new series, so far with an emphasis on commerce, although there is also *listening and note-taking* (which, interestingly, is for the native speaker as well as the foreign student). The books are fairly short, each one is linked to taped material and can be used for self-study. The material seems to be authentic and exercises, eg in *English for bank cashiers*, focus on vocabulary and on the manipulation of structurally different but functionally similar expressions, all within contextualizing dialogues. The units are short and consolidation and reinforcement frequent.

3.3/4 English Studies Series (264) Oxford University Press.

This is one of the older ESP series, the first volume having been published in 1964, the last (apparently), number 11, in 1971. The series is aimed at university students and intends to help them with their reading and writing. All the texts are authentic and unsimplified, chosen from standard textbooks, usually, or from other works which the student might be expected to have to read. The texts are graded by difficulty level and are from a wide range of sub-topics, both to maintain students' interest and to appeal to as many students of a subject as possible. There is also stylistic selection, to use an older approach, in that texts are chosen in order to demonstrate a range of styles, although this can be given a modern interpretation since different texts exemplify different functions, eg definition, explanation, contrast, etc.

Each book follows more or less the same format, although some books have many fewer exercises than others. The texts are generally long and are difficult, which might suggest a high level of English in the students (although many university students have to cope with material much above their competence), but some of the exercises are on 'elementary' points of grammar, eg articles and prepositions. This is deliberate, however, as M J Clarke, author of Books 1 and 2 explains, suggesting that there is a mismatch between what students can read with understanding and what they can write correctly themselves. His exercise material is based on his knowledge of what students commonly get wrong, and it is to be assumed that the authors of the other books in the series are similarly experienced in 'common' mistakes.

The exploitation of the text is according to *explication de texte* as described by Mackay and Mountford (222). Thus very detailed explanations are given of every 'difficult' word and phrase in the text, either as 'Notes' or split into 'Vocabulary' and 'Grammar', normally after the text, although in Book 6 the vocabulary notes come first. This method encourages very intensive reading generally at the word and phrase level, although some of the preoccupations of the *English in Focus* writers, for example implicational meaning, reference items and connectives, are tested and even taught in the comprehension and grammar exercises.

The exercise section generally begins with comprehension work, which can take varying forms not only from book to book but also within each book, ranging from content questions on small details of the text, to a search for the main point of each paragraph to a discussion of the implications or truth value of the text.

The exercises are on both grammar and vocabulary, each developing points in the texts, although most of the practice sentences may not relate to the text or to each other. Vocabulary exercises are generally of the type 'replace a phrase with a single word from the text' and discriminating between near-synonyms. The grammar exercises are a mixture of remedial (generally articles and prepositions: to be inserted in passages from the text) and work on, very commonly, relative clauses, other types of dependent clauses, verb tenses and modal verbs, adverb positions, plus some stylistically more advanced structures, as structures of inversion ('Not only . . ., etc.').

The *English Studies Series* books give the student a lot of information about English vocabulary and grammar (generally at the sentence level or below). (Although one book, 8, *Language teaching texts* by H G Widdowson gives more information about the content of the texts than about their language. His book is also untypical in brevity of the texts and in the low number but greater variety of exercises.) Keys to the exercises are given and the books can be used for self-study. Almost none of the books contain any illustrations or diagrams and the format of many is very dense indeed. They are nonetheless popular perhaps because more familiar than some more recent books. Students feel that they are working hard and learning a lot though perhaps this is more of a general consolidation in English than help with the requirements of their special subject.

3.3/5 Nucleus Series (265) Longman.

The *Nucleus* series was developed in Tabriz, Iran, for use with university students but it is now also used with pupils in the upper forms of secondary schools around the world. The series aims to introduce 'the language learner to uses of English which are essential to scientific and technological communication. It is intended for students with some knowledge of general English, who need to reactivate this knowledge and apply it to the comprehension of written and spoken discourse.' Thus the emphasis is on reading and listening comprehension, and taped listening comprehension material is provided.

The content of the textbooks is organized conceptually in three groupings: description of *form* (which includes properties, location and structure), description of *process*, and *measurement*, the groupings being interwoven for the sake of variety. As Martin Bates writes:

> 'Concepts formed a bridge between the scientific knowledge which the learner had already gained through his own language and the rhetorical resources by means of which this knowledge could be organized and communicated in the foreign language. We decided to begin by teaching the realization of basic scientific concepts in English, since their meaning and relevance were easily recognizable and could be conveyed without the need for metalanguage which the overt teaching of rhetoric demanded.
>
> ... But we felt that a course which concentrated on the overall organization of texts would be a logical sequence to our concept-based course.
>
> The main advantage of using concepts as the basis for selecting our introductory material was that they encouraged language transfer and enabled the student to apply what he had learned to different contexts – linguistic, situational and functional. They were not tied to any particular unit of language, whether lexical, grammatical or rhetorical.' (198)

The similarities with and differences from *English in Focus* can be seen. A second series of *Nucleus* books is envisaged, organized rhetorically.

This conceptual approach has been praised (by S Rixon, reviewing *Nucleus: General Science*, in ESPMENA 9, 1977) as being just what students require when beginning a university course, implying that they have *not* already acquired an adequate conceptual basis for their studies. The approach is not seen to 'poach' on the territory of the subject specialist teacher, however.

Another advantage of the conceptual approach was that it fitted in well with structural grading. The series aims to cover some remedial grammar, and this it does skilfully, although Rixon (above) requests 'grammar headings' to assist the students' consolidation.

An interesting feature of the *Nucleus* series is that it consists of one 'core book' and nine specific books for different subjects, eg Biology, Geology, Physics. This arrangement partly derived from and led to a team method of production, of advantage to teachers and course writers who were non-scientists. The content obviously derives from a study of relevant scientific material, but is not based on any statistical register study.

The components of the series can be used in several ways. The core book (*General Science*) 'presents and practises language which is shared by the various branches of science and technology, including semi-technical lexical items like *diameter*, *ratio*, etc, and items of general use such as *consist*, *depend*, etc, together with essential grammatical items such as passive, sentence connectives, modal verbs, etc'. Each special subject book follows the same conceptual sequence as the core book (eg Unit 1 in each book is 'Properties and shapes', Unit 4 is 'Measurement I'), but uses more specialized language and contains appropriate reading and listening comprehension passages. Thus the core book can precede the study of a special subject book, or the two can be used side by side, or the special subject book can be used alone (although some essential points are presented in more detail in the core book).

Although one of the aims of *Nucleus* is to help reading comprehension, the texts are short (and non-authentic). Reading strategies are not taught as such, students apparently improving their reading by improving their general grasp of English and their knowledge of specialist English.

What *Nucleus* has been greatly, and rightly, praised for (Review of *Nucleus: Biology* by Paul Fanning, *ESPMENA* 7, 1977) is the great number, variety and liveliness of the exercises. There are innumerable drawings and diagrams, involving much 'information transfer'. Most of the grammar and vocabulary practice is related to drawings or diagrams, thus contextualizing it, and all practice sentences relate to each other or to the text. Thus although the skills emphasized are traditionally 'passive', they are practised in an active way. In the process 'a mass of vocabulary' is put across and 'a surprising amount of ground is covered' (Fanning, above). The *Nucleus* books are thus interesting and stimulating for the students and also for the teacher.

3.3/6 Special English Series (266) Collier-Macmillan.

This series is rather similar to *English for Careers* [(261) and Section 3.3/1 above], but each book contains more exercises. The series is aimed at students with 'a good grounding in basic grammar and vocabulary' but who want to improve their English 'within the framework of a technical vocabulary that is of interest . . . either privately or professionally'. Professional areas covered include 'Accounting', 'Advertising', 'Air travel', 'The jet engine', 'Seafaring'.

The books are fairly short and each unit is based on 'conversations which . . . are deliberately written in the colloquial or idiomatic speech used by technicians or specialists as they go about their everyday activities'. This represents an interesting meeting of two dimensions of register analysis: technical vocabulary (often identified with formality) and colloquial or informal speech. It is not clear what the authors' sources of information on register are (although we are told that the 'technical content (is) accurate in every respect') as the dialogues are stilted and unnatural.

Comprehension questions follow the dialogue and then five exercises which drill structure, and test vocabulary (by slot-filling and by 'making up sentences using the vocabulary'). These are all very much 'textbook exercises'. The rationale for the selection of grammatical points is not clear. Some of the books in the series contain photographs of relevant authentic-seeming documents and other realia but there is no attempt to exploit these.

3.3/7 Materials produced by the English Language Teaching Development Unit (ELTDU) ELTDU/OUP.

The materials produced by ELTDU do not form a series, but have certain similarities so can perhaps be treated as a group. The areas covered are in the commercial and technical fields, and are treated in a non-academic way. The materials are altogether more ambitious and interesting than *English for Careers* or *Special English Series*, which cover some of the same professions.

The ELTDU materials are aimed at or near the intermediate level (as tested on the ELTDU Stages of attainment scale and test battery (234)) eg *English for Business: The Bellcrest Series*, which is aimed generally at business-men; *English for secretaries; The case of Harkwood Ltd*, which is for those in financial management; and *The Crisis Series* for those in the technical professions. *English in flight*, which is for air-hostesses, is at the pre-intermediate level, and *Assignment Mornesia*, which is for diplomats, is post-intermediate.

Within the ELTDU materials there is a mixture of very traditional and very modern ideas, a mixture which appears to succeed. Thus each course contains a certain (sometimes quite large) amount of grammatical exercise material including a lot of fairly traditional looking drills, to be done in the classroom, or in the language lab, or with a cassette at home. Texts for background reading or even for the introduction of vocabulary are not authentic: although sometimes the listening comprehension is. However, side by side with the drills we find great use of free-ranging role play exercises and other devices to produce discussion or even confrontation amongst the students.

The materials were designed for particular classes of students and the component parts of each course seem carefully selected and carefully related to each other. Development is often cyclical so that language items and language functions introduced in one part are practised again elsewhere. In order to make the materials suitable for as wide a range of people as possible, presumably, more is included than might be needed by any one class. Thus some revolutions in the cyclical arrangement and some drilling, for example, can be omitted by advanced classes. Part I of each unit in *The case of Harkwood*, for example, consists of programmed units in vocabulary which could be treated as a self-contained course in themselves (or done as homework). A self-study book exists as part of *English for Business: The Bellcrest Series* and could be omitted, or used as extra consolidation, used for homework, etc.

The syllabus for each ELTDU has both grammatical and notional/functional components, the notions and functions being as carefully selected as the grammar (eg in *Assignment Mornesia* such notions as obligation, contingency, promising are featured, and within promising, offering or withholding information, etc, differences of formality and informality, directness and indirectness are considered).

The methods of data collection and selection are not explained by the course writers but although the texts, etc, are not authentic they seem both realistic and relevant. Thus in *English for secretaries* each unit begins, very traditionally, with a 'text' but this text is a memo, or a brochure, ie something that a secretary really might have to read, which is printed to appear like a 'real' memo, etc. Later, writing practice involves letters, reports and memos (some of which involve summarizing, so often practised in an unrelated way, ie not modified to the style of a memo or report, etc). Even such basics as spelling and punctuation are contextualized and presented in letter from the boss to be corrected. Particularly interesting components of the ELTDU materials are the listening comprehension and other language lab work (eg in *English in flight*) and the ideas and materials for role play exercises in all courses.

3.4 Textbooks on Social Science topics

The Social Sciences are poorly represented in ESP, thus perhaps offering proof that school and university students need English to learn Science and Technology rather than subjects in the Humanities or Social Sciences. Various articles exist describing courses to help English-speaking students of arts or social science subjects acquire a reading knowledge of another language, but the equivalent does not seem to exist – or has not appeared in textbook form – for the non-English speaking student. The British Council bibliography lists several books published on the Continent in (mainly) the fields of Law and Economics and which seem to focus on the teaching or listing of vocabulary and on giving of information rather than specifically on the skill of reading.

A few books have been produced on journalism, including one in the *Special English Series*, which is more practically oriented, whereas the others are exemplifying the style of newspaper writing in English for the student on an English literature or English life and culture type of course (eg (283), (284) in the bibliography).

Both the *English in Focus* and *English Studies Series* are represented in the field of Social Science, and are aimed at the more advanced student. Almost nothing exists for the intermediate level student except McArthur, *A rapid course in English for students of Economics* (281). This is a fairly lively book with plenty of general grammar and vocabulary exercises, which are purportedly contextualized although some of them are rather mechanical. The reason for their selection is not entirely clear. Some attention is given to word-building, a preoccupation of the author's and probably useful at the beginning stages of a an academic discipline. The chief aim of the book however is to practise reading comprehension, although the strategies of reading are not discussed and text grammar is not studied. The chief device is to have two versions of each text (not in the later units). At the beginning of the unit there is a very simple text followed by exercises practising some of the language features in it. The unit concludes with a more difficult text on the same subject matter and re-using some of the grammar and vocabulary which has been practised. The texts have been devised by the author (after reading a number of genuine Economics textbooks) and they certainly fulfil his aim of providing contexts for all the language taught. One wonders how typical they are, though, of the kind of reading that Economics students will have to cope with.

A few of the exercises in McArthur make use of diagrammed material. An interesting article by Mead and Lilley (272) suggests that the use of graphs, charts, etc can be of great use in helping to convey some of the complex content of Economics, in providing stimulus for language practice and in motivating students.

3.5 Textbooks on the Physical Sciences

A range of approaches and aims is represented in textbooks in Physical Science. Virtually all, however, with the exception of those produced by the BBC (316), (317) have an academic context, as the scientist is typically academic, perhaps, unlike the technologist or technician. This might earlier have implied a fairly advanced student, both in terms of knowledge of English and knowledge of science, but newer books [*Basic English for Science* (321), Bolitho and Sandler (314) and Royds-Irmak (328)] are intended for the younger pupil, even the beginner.

Most writers say that they have produced a 'language textbook and not a science textbook' (quotation from Bolitho and Sandler), but *Basic English for Science* looks like a textbook for Science for the native speaker even and Royds-Irmak suggests that her book can be taught 'by either the English teacher or by the Science-in-English teacher'. Since science and English may be equally new to some school pupils this may be a good idea [see Newberry (301)]. Most textbooks, however, including *Basic English for Science*, stress that they are not outside the competence of the usual English teacher.

Ewer and Latorre (322) and Croft and Brown (320) both base their selection of material on frequency studies, but the other authors do not give a basis for their selection. There is a high degree of agreement, though on the grammatical items covered, despite the deficiencies of studies of scientific language (see Section 3.2 above). Swales, however, (who has in fact made some analysis of various types of scientific text) does discuss in his introduction to his *Writing Scientific English* (334) some of the commonly accepted views on scientific language and is led to omit the customarily included relative clauses and conditional clauses. At the other end of the scale, Royds-Irmak concentrates excessively on the passive and just a very few other structures.

Swales, Bolitho and Sandler, and *Basic English for Science* contain some mention and practice of some of the functions and notions employed by scientists, and also organize some units around them. Ewer and Latorre, however, is a structurally organized and graded textbook although 'notions' are involved in that the texts chosen to head each unit deal with the philosophy of Science, one of the aims of the course being 'to foster critical scientific thought'.

The selection of texts is obviously a problem since so many topics can be included under the term 'science'. Only Swales gives a reason for limitation ('to the fields of Physics, Chemistry and Engineering because I feel that rather different syntactic and organizational difficulties confront foreign students of Biology, Agriculture, Zoology, etc'); the other books contain texts on a very wide range of topics. This might surely mean that any of these textbooks might be irrelevant for part of the time for some of the students. This is probably not a problem for beginners, though.

Analysis of current publications

Swales' book is aimed specifically at writing, building up from detailed grammar exercises to 'fairly short and fairly straightforward descriptions, explanations and interpretations . . . stopping short of instructing the student how to write technical reports, reviews, discussions or theses'. The exercises are generally textbook-bound but are lively and offer the student an attractive element of choice, eg 'If you think that certain of the following statements are not true, write them out as negative statements. If you think they are true, leave them.' There is also a lot of good practice on such basics as singular versus plural.

Bolitho and Sandler also practise writing and also stop short of full reviews, reports, etc. They too have a good range of exercises, including a number of short exercises spread throughout the book which give practice in verbalizing numbers, symbols, etc, surely useful practice for scientists.

Ewer and Latorre say that the focus of their book is oral, which seems surprising since it is a rather daunting collection of long texts with numerous grammar and vocabulary exercises and explanation. By 'oral' the authors mean that the exercise material should be drilled! Although the exercises are varied, they are nonetheless uncontextualized and in obviously textbook language. Ewer and Latorre's book is a useful fund of information about English for scientists, however, especially in the sections on word study and in the series of appendices. It also provides a good practice in (extensive) reading, since after the series of twelve units, each of which develops the grammar and vocabulary of *one* text, there is a series of eighteen unadapted authentic texts with no exercise material.

The BBC's *Scientifically speaking* might perhaps be thought to introduce spoken language. Its focus is vocabulary, explained in great detail in the textbook, which would be of use to native as well as non-native speaker. The accompanying tapes have a rather artificial story-line and use a journalistic style to introduce information on a variety of scientific topics. There is no opportunity for spoken practice, however.

The focus of Smithies (330) is reading, since he believes that this is the chief activity of many Science students. His aim is to 'practise close textual reading requiring that the student make deductions and draw logical conclusions' (this presumably considered as the prerogative of the scientist). The reading is certainly 'close', since as many as twenty questions may be asked on twenty lines of print. A number of the comprehension questions relate to vocabulary, although Smithies has said that this is *not* what he is concerned with. 'Too often a student limits his comprehension to vocabulary items which he strings together and hopes will make sense.' It is structure, however, which is important and which 'our material sets out to test and explain'. Certainly we must acknowledge that Smithies does have many good questions on (textual) structure, dealing, amongst other things, with connectives. His book is self-study, multiple-choice, with all the answers, including the incorrect ones, explained. The texts vary greatly in subject matter and style (some very journalistic and culture-bound), though they are graded for complexity. All are authentic. A review (331) of Smithies wonders why the multiple-choice method is used exclusively, suggesting a variation with true/false questions, and some tasks, eg completing diagrams, filling in summary charts, etc.

A failure to use more active exercise types is also a criticism of Royds-Irmak [reviewed (329)]. Royds-Irmak is a general course book with very mechanical, unrelated exercises on vocabulary and grammar, and no focus on any particular skill. At the end of each unit, however, there are very interesting, but unexploited, suggestions for further activities. There is no apparent grading in the book and each of the many units has an identical formula. This involves the initial comparison of two texts, A in 'ordinary language' and B in 'scientific language' – both with the same subject matter. The 'different in form but similar in meaning' words and phrases are subsequently discussed. However, text B is in no way particularly scientific, the differences being if anything due to level of formality. Frequently there are no *significant* differences and too often both texts are awkwardly written if not completely unnatural.

A word must be said finally about Mathematics, the most difficult of the sciences to practise since it is essentially not textual. Sturgess (333) is basically a reference book listing typical phrases for the expression of scientific statements. Some mathematical material is contained in Price (327), which is organized like a thesaurus, but with extensive charting of grammatical details.

3.6 Textbooks on Technology

ESP materials on Technology can be legitimately located in both EAP and EOP. Thus Engineering as a subject of study in higher education is catered for by several textbooks with an academic bias. The practical language needs of the 'engineer on the job' as well as of other technical workers are also supplied by a number of publications, although yet more would be welcome. Since technological and technical subjects – even at university – should surely be practical, insufficient material of a practical nature is available.

Within the academic area new development, as with Science, seems to be for the beginners' level, hitherto rather neglected. Thus Beardwood *et al* (362) present a carefully organized structurally sequenced book with a very limited structural syllabus, providing for plenty of practice and repetition and utilizing all the skills. The units are a mixture of topical and notional. The great problem in such a course is the large amount of vocabulary to be covered. This seems to be adequately coped with. Particularly good points are the 'language notes' which are often pictorial and serve to highlight key language areas, peculiarities of spelling and pronunciation, etc. Also valuable is the large amount of practice – written and spoken – in the use of numbers, formulae, etc, essential for technicians. As in *Nucleus* there are a great many illustrations, all with exercises based on them.

Methold and Waters (378) is also for the elementary student and also presents carefully controlled vocabulary and grammar work. Many illustrations again are used, but these are more purely illustrative and active language work is not based on them.

For the more advanced students emphasis is very often on vocabulary and reading eg Brasnett (364), who gives very careful explanations of vocabulary especially of those items which have a non-technical as well as a technical use, and Hawkey (372) who for some reason focuses on a very varied list of vocabulary, ranging, for example, from *chassis* to *maintain* and *exceed*. McAllister and Madama (377) have produced a very dense, encyclopedic text, emphasizing word for word study and the understanding of grammatical rules intended for the (presumably very diligent) self-study student.

In addition a number of other readers for the technologist are available, eg (382), (383), (385). Practice in writing for the academic technologist is not completely lacking, however, as writing and reading practice are provided by volumes in the *English in Focus* series [(370), (379), (381), see Section 3.4 above.] Drobnic (345) and Mackay and Mountford (350) both describe reading and writing programmes. Listening and speaking are focused on by Coveney (343).

Turning to EOP we note that listening and speaking are focused on almost entirely, which is what we might expect. Thus Hodlin *et al* (374) is entirely oral, being a low level course for overseas staff in hospital laundries, aiming 'to teach the English the learner needs for his immediate job' and 'to teach the English needed for simple social contact within the work place between the learner and native English-speaking workers'. The course is to be taught in the hospital in work time. A taped component is included and also slides and flashcards.

English in flight (ELTDU) (368) is a course for air hostesses which 'concentrates on training the student both to understand and to produce the type of spoken English that is required. The skills of reading and writing English are not dealt with as they are largely irrelevant to the work of the hostess'. As with other ELTDU materials a great deal of listening and speaking practice is provided, bringing in much vocabulary and grammar practice, but organized situationally and functionally, building up to role play.

The Crisis Series (ELTDU) (369) is 'designed for use with professional technical people of or near managerial status' who are 'increasingly required to represent their organizations in contacts with counterparts from other countries'. Their work involves learning about, explaining and discussing technical projects, and selling products. Thus the course has 'a definite emphasis on oral/aural skills'. It is organized as a series of assignments, with the students simulating the roles of a 'putative team of technical trouble-shooters'. Reading, however, is involved, as students have to read and process the information from a number of different types of document – combining this with aural information –

before getting together to discuss crisis action, to suggest solutions to problems, to argue alternatives, etc.

Such work is obviously 'active', yet the methods used are not unique to the learning and practising of technology, nor is any use made of technology, beyond that of the tape-recorder. One might expect that courses for practising technologists be more media and materials oriented.

Programmed learning, using linear-programmed instruction, together, presumably, with tapes and slides, is provided by the *Tutor-Tape Audio-Visual Technical Series* (387) although this is in fact intended for the native learner. *North Sea challenge* (386) is a language pack produced by Linguistics Systems Engineering and BP Educational Service, but it is nonetheless document-based and relates more to talking than to doing.

Much work of interest in Technology, particularly EOP, is described only in articles and has not resulted in textbooks, eg Bodley (337), Coutts (342). As some of this would seem to be more activity based than what has been described above, further description and exemplification would be welcome. Much still obviously remains to be done in the provision of appropriate back-up materials for an activity based language for technology course.

3.7 Textbooks on Medicine

As with textbooks on Science and Technology, we find that textbooks on Medicine published in Britain are mostly general grammar consolidation (with or without vocabulary work) or skill specific – here reading – with very little on listening or speaking.

Thus Austin and Crosfield (396) is a very traditionally conceived book for the elementary student of English (though with apparently some knowledge of nursing) concentrating on grammar and vocabulary with many drills (not always contextualized).

Parkinson (408) is very specifically aimed for doctors and nurses 'intending to work in Britain . . . or any country where English is used in the hospital' but rather than helping with oral/aural skills the aim is to activate the students' dormant knowledge of English grammar learnt 'at some time of their life' but not subsequently used. 'The book deals with the points of the language which cause difficulties for nearly all non-English speaking people' (presumably in the author's experience). Thus each unit deals with one grammatical point which is first exemplified in a short dialogue 'of everyday English frequently heard in hospital'. These dialogues appear realistic, but no source is given for them. After the dialogue is an explanation of the grammar point, followed by a large number of further examples of its use in apparently fairly authentic language, thus providing a good amount of contextualization. There are no exercises. This type of reference grammar would appear to be useful, especially if the grammar 'is explained in the simplest possible way, with the minimum of grammatical terms'. (The author does not always succeed in this.) However there is no index or even table of contents, so that items are very hard to locate. The units are extremely varied in length, the one on verb tenses being excessively long and perhaps confusing. There is useful material on often-confused words, though, eg *bring*, *fetch*, *take*.

Parkinson (407) is better organized for reference and is a mixture of essential information for doctors coming to work in Britain (eg a detailed chapter on the National Health Service) and an explanation and listing of useful language material, for example colloquialisms for parts of the body which doctors might encounter. (A section on idioms using parts of the body would seem to have doubtful practical value, though, for the specific contexts envisaged.)

Horzella and Labarca is not available in Britain but in a review of it (*ESPMENA* 4, 1976) Swales praises its new exercise types, which focus on aspects of the interpretation of written texts.

Brasnett (398) and Methold and Methold (405) are both primarily reading courses, aimed at pre-medical students. Each gives the opportunity for extensive as well as intensive reading. This has been praised by Fanning (406): 'ESP would be greatly facilitated if students had greater access to reading materials that broadened their experience of technical English while sustaining their morale at the same time'

– ie 'something in between a textbook of anatomy and Agatha Christie.'

Brasnett organizes his book into series of short texts on the same topic, interspersed with exercises on grammar and vocabulary. Fanning (399) praises this arrangement as a series of contexts are provided to reinforce the new vocabulary and because the real life study situation would involve the reading of a text several passages long, not one short comprehension passage. At the beginning of the book Brasnett uses the same idea as Royds-Irmak (see Section 3.5 above) of two texts on the same topic, one more technical than the other, but the two versions are more realistic this time, it being recognized that phrase to phrase or sentence to sentence equivalence cannot be maintained.

Brasnett's exercise material is thorough if a little unvaried in format but one of the most valuable features is the extensive discussion and exercising of such things as using a catalogue and an index, meanings of punctuation, use of abbreviations, etc – very useful study skills aid.

Methold and Methold's focus is on comprehension. They provide a glossary of difficult words, true/false comprehension questions and vocabulary exercises. Comprehension is *taught* however by means of rewriting exercises (chiefly paraphrasing) in which students are asked to examine and work with typical and typically difficult (according to the authors) examples of written medical English. (Many are surely just features of formal written style.) It is hoped that through working on these difficult structures, students will be able to understand them when encountered in a reading. This seems a valuable idea, although occasionally the mechanics of the exercise seem more difficult than the structure practised. Additional exercises are on summarizing and/or translation.

Although Parkinson's work is for foreign doctors and nurses in Britain, it does not help them converse. This gap is filled by the work of Candlin *et al* (400). DOPACS is extremely carefully worked out and based on considerable research (see Candlin *et al* (389)). The written material of DOPACS is supported by audio-tapes and visuals and looks at non-linguistic as well as linguistic behaviour. Each of 24 units is focused on a micro-function (see Candlin *et al* (454)) which is demonstrated, before students are given both recognition and production practice. The material is carefully controlled, the objectives are made very clear, and the student is tested at the end of each unit. The listening material contains several interesting exercise types, similar to those in *English in flight* (see Section 3.3/7 above).

Some of the most interesting work in medical English is not in textbook form and could not be. This is the work of Allwright and Allwright (388) and Currie *et al* (390). This work involves a diagnostic approach where students' needs are revealed in spontaneous (or nearly so) interactions. These interactions are prepared by means of a study of actual cases (partly studied in the language lab) followed by a 'case conference' in which the students (all qualified doctors) exchange views. The activities are directed as much as possible by the students. The only long-term preparation can be in the work of collecting input data – authentic texts and recordings – for possible use by the students later.

3.8 Textbooks on commercial topics

There is a large number of textbooks in the area of commerce, most particularly in the general area of office practice and business. The more interesting publications have been discussed above (3.3/7). A great many of the remainder are general in all senses, ie they are intended for beginners or near-beginners and pursue the traditional structural syllabus, practising all skills, employing an invented story-line and being very much confined to the classroom, the only 'business' element being a veneer of vocabulary and the choice of some (not all) of the situations. Examples are Beesley (414), Pearson (445) and de Schriffin *et al* (447). *Modern Office Ltd* (417) is more lively than some and does make use of different kinds of document type-invoice, memo, etc.

For the more advanced student the trend in ESP is for books which closely resemble those produced for the native speaker [eg Woolcott and Unwin (451)], some being offered by the publishers as being suitable for both (eg Stanwell and Swift (450) and Parsons and Hughes (444). This seems a good idea, but more attention needs to be given to the brief, clear and relevant explanation and practice of grammatical features for the foreign student. (The native speaker could also use a more accurate and relevant explanation of language points than is customarily given.)

Intermediate level books designed specifically for the foreign student include Mack (435) which focuses on vocabulary in a very artificial way with the minimum of exercise material, and Howatt *et al* (432) which has links with the ELTDU materials (see Section 3.3/7 above), a range of materials being provided (class texts, reading texts, programmed units) to be used as required.

Considering skill selective courses we find reading comprehension courses, often based primarily on texts from *The Economist* eg Fisher (430) and Binham (415), both of which also incorporate vocabulary and grammar practice, and the writing of reports, summaries, etc. Fisher manages to relate the writing exercises more closely to the reading passages.

Very often it is assumed, however, that the student of commerce already knows how to perform such writing operations as the production of a report or a summary or a set of minutes and merely needs to be told at the end of the unit to do it. A great deal could be done on the mechanics of such writing, linking it to strategies of note-taking and listening comprehension work.

What writing is taught is confined to business letters. *Commercial correspondence* (422) is very much for the foreign student, concentrating on details of layout and basic grammar points. Business letters can be linguistically very complex, however, so that a very large amount of demonstration and practice (in different styles and exemplifying different functions) is required. This is provided by Spooner and McKellan (449), using a story line approach, and Kench (433) using sequences of related letters.

3.9 Materials for study skills or EAP (English for Academic Purposes)

This is as yet an underdeveloped area in ESP, at least in terms of published textbooks. No study skills materials are listed in the first edition of the British Council Information Guide on ESP (April 1976) and only six items appear in the supplement (1978).

As is evident from the work in EST, large numbers of pupils in school and students at university and college are using English as their language of study. Too often they have not mastered adequate techniques for study in their own language, and so have no skill to transfer to English.

A skill has to be mastered: it cannot simply be explained, but must also be extensively practised. Thus Purvis (492) is valuable for the numerous and varied exercises for the practice of note-taking which are provided. A great many short texts are used for practice – first with single paragraphs and later with series of connected paragraphs. A number of note-taking techniques are explained and practised and the students encouraged to perfect their own set of chosen techniques. (There is also a very clear, colour-coded teacher's manual.)

Note-taking is not necessarily an academic skill but is also used by secretaries and other people in commercial situations. Ferguson and O'Reilly (485) seem to provide more generally applicable practice than Purvis, and involve spoken input as well as written. Their book is also thought useful for the native speaker, study skills being an area where the needs of foreign- and native-speaker can overlap.

A problem with study skills is that of subject matter. The skills are not subject-specific and the typical class for which many materials have been prepared consists of students pursuing many different special subjects [see British Council, 1978c (51)]. One solution is to base the practice material on the subject of studying itself as in Heaton (486) and Candlin *et al* (483). These are both very well prepared and thorough courses, but ultimately rather dull because restricted to the same subject matter, which tends to pall even on students of Education. Other solutions are to have a range of different topics, as in Ferguson and O'Reilly or Wallace (495), or to aim the course at a restricted set of subjects, as Purvis (Science and Medicine, although the texts used are generally interesting and easy enough to appeal to a wider range than this). An ingenious solution is found by Plaister (490) all of whose units are on different aspects of the mythical Kingdom of Kochen, although in fact this would seem to appeal primarily to Social Science students (perhaps also some Technology students) as the units cover such things as the monarchy, foreign investment, religion, agriculture and transport. The material in Plaister is 'designed to simulate, as closely as possible, a university lecture' and there is extensive practice on lecture listening (as well as much general vocabulary and grammar work).

Authentic lectures have been recorded and extracted from by McDonough (499) in a series of tapes and exercises which aims to cover most of the spectrum of university subjects.

Listening to lectures and note-taking, however, do not exhaust the range of study skills and Yorkey (496) and Wallace (495) aim to cover much more than this, including reading strategies (Yorkey), use of the library, essay and thesis planning and writing, and elements of grammar and writing (Wallace). Both books have much useful information about the nature of academic work and some relevant and authentic-seeming exercises, but both books probably try to cover too much. Several of their component sections could be made into separate courses.

The skill of reading, which is after all a study skill, has been much practised in the different specialist subject areas. More could be done for extensive reading, and the use of general academic material explored, rather than material which is too narrowly subject specific.

Similarly in the area of writing, which, compared to reading, is much neglected. Even such writing courses as there are generally involve so much grammar work or reading that little opportunity for writing is left. Even more than for reading, the academic nature of writing is common to a range of special subjects. Thus the functions of definition, classification, generalization, etc, so often studied in relation to EST are surely the functions of any piece of academic writing, whatever the subject matter.

Much work is going on in study skills and considerable research has been done (too often uncompleted, however). But most of this work, if accessible, is in the form of articles, not coursebooks. Freeman (460) for example, suggests a large number of exercises, few of which have been utilized. Much basic research requires to be undertaken into exactly what are the skills and microskills involved in studying, and into how generalizable material to practise them can be, but meanwhile articles on related materials could be compared and possibly some more permanent courses produced.

3.10 Concluding remarks

3.10/1 *The communicative approach*
As can be seen, both structural and notional/functional/communicative approaches have been adopted in the preparation of ESP textbooks. ESP is thought by many to belong more appropriately to the communicative approach. Some articles explain very clearly how to set about the preparation of a would-be communicative course but more can be done on the development and explanation of exercise types and other practice materials.

Ultimately, however, there is surely a logical error in the communicative approach in that real communication takes place in unique situations, so that one cannot generalize nor try to reproduce a previous success. One can only prepare the setting for a communicative event but cannot predict that it will occur.

3.10/2 *Grammar*
Many of the books discussed have a large grammatical component, often of a general nature. The extent of specialist grammar is not established but many course writers have their own set of working assumptions. More clarification would be welcome, as for example, on the passive, assumed by everyone to be an essential feature of scientific writing. As has been pointed out, however, by Strevens (81) and Lee Kok Cheong (371), introduction of the passive rarely explains *why* it is used in Science, or even gives a completely accurate grammatical description of it. A point for investigation is how much explicit information about language students need to be given, it being often assumed that Science students, in particular, welcome detailed grammatical discussion. More work could be done on the production of interesting modes of grammatical explanation, eg pictorial as in Beardwood *et al* (362).

3.10/3 Vocabulary

Vocabulary is obviously a key issue in ESP and some courses are based exclusively on it. Specialized dictionaries and reference works are clearly of use, especially to translators and those requiring only a reading knowledge of a language. Coursebooks, however, especially for in-service students, perhaps do not need to concentrate on the very specialized vocabulary items as students will get these from other sources. Rather it if the sub-technical level which is often difficult. Thus Edwards (391), teaching midwives and nurses, suggested that 'esoteric terms' were explained by the subject teachers, whereas she should concentrate on 'giving the students a good grounding in the vocabulary which it will be taken for granted they know'. Martin (474) distinguishes 'academic vocabulary' which is 'sub-technical', occurs across disciplines, is often incorrectly used by students, but rarely recognized as a problem. Perhaps Phillips *et al* (353) are referring to the same thing when they distinguish 'organization of knowledge' verbs: 'those procedural verbs the primary function of which is to articulate the development of an idea in a discourse', for example *examine, ascertain, determine*. Phillips *et al* found in a study of four agriculture textbooks that only about 15% of verbs were specifically associated with agriculture, whereas 60–70% were 'semi-technical', ie generally applicable to Science, and the remainder were, as they termed them, verbs for the 'organization of knowledge'.

Fanning (365) suggests that it is not single words which are always difficult, but phrases, so that common combinations of words should be taught, not just the individual vocabulary items of a discipline. Methods of teaching, testing and rehearsing vocabulary vary greatly, too few managing to reach a free-practice situation. A problem, especially with lower level students is having to introduce a large number of vocabulary items at once. Too often this is done by means of a generally very artificial text. Only in *The case of Harkwood* (424) is the method of programmed instruction used (and revealingly discussed).

3.10/4 Reading

Of the four skills, reading is the one most often dealt with in isolation.

This is an area of continuing interest, though now the focus seems to be moving towards more general or common core reading courses. Although most work on discourse structure has been done within EST, texts from a greater range of academic disciplines could be considered in the same way. The range of straoegies to be employed by all university students, for example, is perhaps the same, regardless of the particular subject-matter, especially if we consider the specific vocabulary as a separate (perhaps minor) issue (see 3.10/3 above).

It can be seen that a great many textbooks use a reading passage as a means of beginning a unit in a general grammar and vocabulary course, and derive the language points to be taught from it. The passage is usually, though not always, specially contrived for the purpose. Most of the material within such a passage is well within the learner's competence and thus the normal reading situation of many students is not reproduced. If the course does not aim to teach reading comprehension as such, then the use of a text in order to contextualize vocabulary and structures, rather than to teach reading strategies, should perhaps not be criticized – though one might note that some supposedly aural-oral courses seem to require students to spend an inordinate amount of time working their way through reading passages.

However, even those courses which aim to cultivate strategies of reading comprehension have been found deficient in some respects. It seems clear that enough is still not known about the nature of the reading process and of ways to improve reading performance. The general reader as well as the occupation or education specific student would benefit from new research into reading.

Even those courses which aim to cultivate strategies of comprehension have been found deficient in some respects. More can usefully be done and in the study skills area, in particular, linking reading to devices for note-taking, exercises in data selection and collection.

Meanwhile we might note that some study skills exercises for 'active reading' could be used for general and non-academic reading. Exercises in data selection and collection, note-taking, the filling in of charts and tables need not be the prerogative of the academic student alone.

3.10/5 ESP and ELT

Most of the criticisms of ESP relate to them as coursebooks in English for the foreign learner rather than as specifically ESP books. We are reminded that ESP is a branch of ELT and perhaps not so different from it as might be supposed. The higher expectations of ESP make more demands on coursebooks, and although the needs of the learner are in many cases more clearly specified, this does not mean that strategies for satisfying them are yet perfected.

There are comparatively few reviews of most of the textbooks referred to and more discussion of their use might be valuable. It is noteworthy though, that almost none of the reviewers looked at had used the textbooks in quite the ways intended, for a variety of reasons. Bates (198) emphasizes that the writer of ESP materials has to make many compromises. Perhaps, too, the teacher has to – in order to make his material seem as specific as possible to his class. Thus as well as textbooks, the teacher needs to be armed with additional materials for the use of his particular class. (See Phillips and Shettlesworth (208).) Monolithic textbooks need to be supplemented or even replaced by packs or selections of material, often realia, providing a range of choice for teacher and pupils.

In some cases we have noted that ESP notebooks have also been thought suitable for the native speaker, and *vice versa*. This is understandable given that the ESP student's goal is often to perform the same job role as a native speaker. Even the native speaker, when learning a new trade or profession has a certain amount of work to do on the language of his job. The use of such joint materials could perhaps be usefully further explored.

Appendix I. Implications for teacher training

A serious problem for ESP in many parts of the world lies in the provision of an adequate supply of teachers. In most cases the people teaching and administering ESP programmes have themselves received no special training in ESP. Most participants at an ESP seminar in Manila in 1978 were 'university teachers who had found themselves thrust, willy-nilly, into ESP and service-English programmes in their institutions'.

Swales (231) notes a common pattern of development in overseas university English departments from the provision of a general English course which is then supplemented with some subject specific reading matter, to the adoption of a commercially produced ESP textbook, to the final situation where each department writes ESP materials itself.

Since they would originally have been recruited to teach the general English course it is likely that many of the teachers would have a traditional literary background. Even though, as Swales (232) notes 'the number of people in the Middle East with recognized TEFL/Applied Linguistics qualifications has increased markedly in recent years', their training may not have included a component on ESP teaching.

Moody (164) reporting on the responses to a questionnaire on ESP courses throughout SE Asia notes that English department teachers are generally academically trained (meaning, presumably, in the literary tradition) and suggests that there is an argument for a 'conversion course' to methods of materials-writing and teaching for ESP.

Judging from the numerous articles about the production of ESP materials at individual departments and institutions which have changed from providing a general English course to an ESP course, this work of materials production is normally undertaken by enthusiastic native speaker expatriates and not by local teachers. (Although in Chile and Colombia local teachers are more involved in ESP programmes.) Swales (231) comments that many Third World English teachers are bored by Science and not sympathetic to its special linguistic features. When asked to teach EST they experience 'a crisis of confidence' and tend to treat a scientific text as they would a literary one, ignoring many relevant and useful types of exploitation. A report on the situation in Thailand (35) notes that most English teachers have no Science background and that 'Teachers who have been trained in general English courses are reluctant or feel uneasy about teaching EST.'

An important component, then, in any teacher training for ESP programme must be directed towards changing the attitude of the teachers towards Science, in particular, and towards some of the other subject specialisms, this change of attitude being particularly vital for the local teachers.

The most fully developed ESP teacher training programme must be that run by J R Ewer in Chile for EST and which he has described in some detail (229). Ewer suggests that there are five problems for teachers when considering teaching EST, including the problem of attitude already mentioned. One problem is conceptual, namely that most teachers of English will not know or understand the concepts of Science. A third problem is a linguistic one since although the teacher is familiar with 'general English' he will not be familiar with the special lexical and structural features of scientific English. Fourthly, Ewer suggests that there may be a problem with methodology as most EST courses are concentrated at the late secondary or tertiary level whereas many teachers will have been trained to teach younger pupils. Finally there is the organizational problem of how to set up an EST programme.

The teacher training programme described by Ewer lasts for 120 hours and is for both practising teachers and undergraduates. The trainees' 'conceptual vacuum' is filled in by readings on Science and Technology, by visits to scientific and technological institutions, and by the building up of portfolios of informative material and visual aids. A slightly larger part of the teacher-training programme is devoted to studying the language of Science, including symbols and abbreviations. The other parts of the course are on methodology and on the organization and administration of an EST programme, including budgeting [see also Ewer (227)].

An important element of the course is the patience and sympathy of the course instructors. Ewer writes that:

> 'One of the first points to emerge from the earlier and shorter versions of the course was the necessity of having enough time to enable the students both to overcome their initial fear of Science and to absorb the many novel aspects of this type of teaching without undue pressure; in particular to develop the realization that they were not only perfectly capable of understanding very broadly what the main branches of science were about and how the scientific and technological mind worked, but that this could be an interesting and enjoyable activity in itself'

The programme described by Ewer has been conducted at a number of institutions in Chile and has since incorporated some study of the special features of Economics and Commerce, as well as EST. Other institutions offering initial training and/or conversion courses in ESP seem few in number, although The British Council/ODM report (40) urges the provision of more courses in Britain and the support of local courses in other parts of the world.

The University of Mosul in Iraq has an M A programme in the teaching of ESP, which largely concentrates on the language of Science and the methodology of teaching Science (alongside the usual components of a course in Applied Linguistics).

The report of the working party on the training of teachers for ESP at the second Isfahan Conference on ESP (27) also concentrated attention on the study of Science within a general Applied Linguistics programme. The working party recommended that the trainees should have lectures on scientific data and methodology, taught by the subject specialist lecturers themselves. In addition the trainees should do some practical work, eg make some laboratory experiments, then tabulate the results, write up a report, etc.

Contact with subject specialist lecturers is also urged by Hughes-Davies (181) and by Davies (268). Davies is writing about a course in International Economics for Swedish students, a course which involves the study of business English and an English textbook on Economic Geography alongside the study of Economics in Swedish. Davies writes that:

> 'It is clear that teacher training is essential if such integrated courses are to function efficiently; language teachers should ideally follow the same business courses as their pupils, while specialist teachers must achieve at least communicative competence in two languages if they are not to be at a disadvantage compared with their pupils.'

Davies writes that he himself enjoyed learning about Economic Geography and did not find it too difficult. It is clear from what he writes, however, that his suggestions involve expenditure of time and effort on the part of language teachers (and also the specialist subject teachers) if they are to keep pace with their pupils. Time is needed not only to study the textbook in Economic Geography, or whatever, but also to produce suitable language learning materials from it.

A knowledge of how to produce language materials from a subject specialist text is surely as important for the teacher of ESP as the ability and enthusiasm to approach and understand the specialist text. Ewer's course in Chile has a component on materials production, but it does not seem to be included in the Mosul programme or in the Isfahan suggestions.

Appendix II. Testing and evaluation

A component of ESP courses which has not yet been fully developed is that of testing and evaluation. Indeed some proponents of ESP claim that testing is inappropriate. Thus in a discussion following the Bogota Seminar in 1977:

> 'H G Widdowson commented that, following the communicative approach, testing was not a normal communicative activity. Imposing tests on learners, therefore, may have the effect of compromising the naturalness of behaviour which the communicative approach aims to promote.' (47)

Elsewhere, however, Widdowson and others, would appear to agree with Ewer (235) that ESP is 'task-oriented' and thus a student on an ESP course is tested when he is asked to perform the task for which the ESP course has prepared him. This kind of test may be essentially informal. The Bogota Seminar (47) also reports that:

> 'T C Jupp commented that . . . testing of English skills in an employment situation is done by the workers' supervisors without their being aware of being tested.'

Other ESP course directors, for example Higgens and Davis (253) have found the need for more explicit tests, however:

> 'There was a need felt for weekly objective feedback to students. This would have helped them evaluate their progress and to see in which skill they needed to concentrate most at that time. However, in the context of study skills, it is not clear what form such an assessment might take.'

The only completely worked out system of testing within an ESP situation is the ELTDU Stages of attainment scale and test battery (234). This consists of a scale of eight stages (J–H) of language attainment which can be used to define language level 'not only in linguistic terms, but also in terms of what tasks employees at particular stages can be expected to perform with the language at their disposal'. Once an employee has been placed on the scale an employer can know which tasks he can be asked to perform (and with what degree of competence) and a teacher can know what further types of training would be required. A person is placed on the attainment scale by means of the test battery. This consists first of a pre-selection test which will indicate the testee's approximate stage of attainment. If a more detailed assessment of language ability is required, then one of three stage tests will be administered. As well as being selection and placement tests, the stage tests can also be used to assess attainment at the end of a language training scheme. The stages of attainment can also be used to define the objectives of a course.

The 1978 British Council Seminar on ESP course design at Dunford House (42), although primarily devoted to the analysis of needs and to syllabus design, also included a short phase on assessment/evaluation. The brief for participants was to derive evaluation instruments directly from the output of a Munbyan specification of needs, not from the materials of a course. Participants prepared tests on particular (Munbyan) micro-skills. It is to be hoped that the proposed seminar publication will contain more details of such tests and of their rationale.

In view of the concurrent rise to prominence of a systems approach to language learning it is surprising that more ESP courses do not have an inbuilt evaluation and testing component. It seems that ESP course designers concentrate their attention at the materials production stage and perhaps lack the energy to go further [see Abbott (197)]. Alderson *et al*, however, suggest five stages in the production of an ESP course (175); needs analysis, syllabus design, materials production, the teaching/learning process, evaluation. Perry (184) describing the systems approach to language learning in the Canadian armed forces suggests the following model:

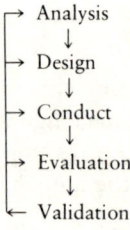

Perry considers that any training programme needs 'clearly defined performance objectives and valid standards of measurement'. The performance objectives for the French-speaking armed forces personnel that Perry was involved with were devised after consultation with potential employers. A profile of each job was built up with each of the four skills allocated on a five-point scale according to level of required proficiency. The evaluation consisted of an initial placement test, a mid-course test, and an end of course test, together with ongoing personal assessment by teaching staff. Validation took the form of questionnaires administered to the students themselves, to the language teachers, to the military instructors, and to military supervisors.

Clearly a well worked out course of instruction should presuppose effective methods of evaluation. If so much effort is expended on preparing a course, some sort of check on its value and success should not be omitted. We must, however, distinguish between tests of the students on the course or evaluations of the course itself.

In his introduction to Oskarsson (256) Trim suggests a fourfold purpose for tests (of students): placement, progress, achievement and proficiency. Ewer, discussing evaluation in EST programmes (235), proposes an initial placement/exemption test, which should be long and global and similar to the end of course test (in order to exempt correctly those who do not need to follow the course). Next there should be periodic modular achievement tests. Finally it is possible that a terminal global achievement examination is needed, because many teaching and educational systems demand it. In addition Ewer suggests that many EST courses abroad smould help to prepare students to take such general proficiency tests as the Davies and TOEFL tests.

As to the content of his tests, Ewer suggests that

> 'Evaluation in the STTE programme is . . . "task"-oriented: its object is to test the various *skills* required by the student, together with the main *linguistic elements* needed in deploying those skills, using *concepts of Science and Technology* with which the student may reasonably be assumed to be familiar at the time of testing.'

Such popular components of traditional English language tests as phonology, Ewer suggests may reasonably be omitted from STTE (scientific, technical and technological English) tests. What he offers as an EST test, however, still sounds more language-oriented (albeit using scientific language) than one might expect from the term 'task-oriented' – which conjures up pictures of the students manufacturing artefacts on consultation of written instructions, performing complicated manoeuvres on receipt of oral instructions, etc. Ewer does not, in fact, detail what exactly his tests would consist of.

A slightly more activity based type of test is suggested by Bianchi (411) when she writes that 'One is concerned with reproducing as nearly as possible the situation in which the participant may find himself.' She suggests the use of realia as much as possible and notes that written tests are a problem.

Vance (236), however, describes an actual test used to place freshman students at Kuwait University into one of two courses on scientific English. A general English placement test had been found to be unsatisfactory since many students who performed well in it nonetheless found themselves subsequently unable to handle the Science-oriented material taught on their course. Hence a new test was devised which 'tested structures, vocabulary and "relationships" (sequencing, cause-effect ... etc) commonly found in English Science materials. We felt the need to test basic knowledge of some scientific relationships, concepts and frames of thinking common to all higher education.' In addition a cloze test using a scientific passage was included and a writing sample based on a diagram.

The new placement test was found to be highly effective and subsequently an exemption test was developed. Vance concludes that:

> 'Though the field of testing for scientific English must be relatively new, there is an obvious need for further development. Our experience cannot be unique... In the same way that the need for specialized English became apparent, so the need for specialized placement testing has become apparent.'

Tan San Yee (194) describing a proposed syllabus for a course for Engineering students suggests that 'a systems approach to syllabus design requires three phases of evaluation (of a course)'. The first phase is before the course begins and amounts to an analysis of students' needs and abilities and an assessment of available resources (teachers, administrators, funds). The second phase is that of 'formative evaluation', ie how the material or programme is being received. The third and final phase occurs after the end of the course and aims to establish its degree of success. Tan San Yee suggests that both subjective and objective methods of evaluation are of value and advocates the use of rating scales and questionnaires for staff and student reactions, the use of the personal impressions of evaluators and the use of a test.

One of the most thorough surveys of different methods of assessment is made by Oskarsson (256). As he is concerned with self-assessment, however, his work might more appropriately be considered in Appendix III along with other aspects of self-directed learning.

We might conclude with a final comment from the Dunford House ESP Seminar Report (42):

> 'New syllabuses and procedures demand new approaches to evaluation. It is clear that many ESP courses do not have an inbuilt component for testing or evaluation. More research and more production needs to be done in this area and the question of whether ESP requires special types of testing and evaluation needs to be tackled.'

Appendix III. Self-directed learning and self-assessment

It was suggested earlier (page 12) that the true ESP course might have only one student in it since it might be found that, even in a class of students supposedly involved in the same specialist area, each student had individual needs and abilities. A logical development of such a situation would be the provision of some form of individualization or self-instruction. Thus Higgens and Davis (253) writing about a pre-sessional course in EAP discovered that even though all their students had the same broad objective, namely advanced study in the UK, and even though the students had been 'filtered' through an initial test of ability there was 'a surprisingly wide range of ability in the basic study skills.' Since, additionally, grouping of the students by field of interest and type of course to be subsequently followed concealed 'considerable differences of individual level', a type of individualized programme was devised.

Individualization of learning had developed separately from ESP, but a number of people are beginning to see a connection between the two, not least because each can utilize a systems approach. In addition both individualization and ESP are commonly thought of in relation to adults. (See page 9 for discussion of the connection of ESP with adult learners and see Grittner (251) on individualization in the school system.)

The most extensive study of individualization in relation to language teaching (not necessarily LSP, however) has been done by CRAPEL [see Henner-Stanchina (252)]. The term used by CRAPEL is *autonomous learning*, and the strategy of autonomous learning was established to cater for those (adult) students who could not come to regular classes because of family or business commitments, distance, aversion to the normal classroom atmosphere, or because of the urgency of their need for a very concentrated course. Once established, however, the autonomous learning strategy has been applied in various situations, including regular evening classes, but also with groups doing ESP in industry.

Stanchina defines autonomy as 'a learner-centred strategy independent of the classroom, where the learner determines his own working conditions, and periodically meets with a helper'. She also writes [quoted in Dickinson (244)]:

> 'Autonomy is an experiment in how learning can be freed from the bounds of any institution, and in how the individual can reclaim control of and responsibility for his or her own education, while investigating the opportunities to learn from a variety of authentic sources.'

Important features of the CRAPEL strategy, as described by Dickinson, are that the learner determines his own goals, his own mode of learning, the materials he will use and his pace of working. He will also monitor his own performance and evaluate his own proficiency.

Consideration of these different features leads Dickinson to attempt to clarify the many terms now current, such as autonomy, self-directed learning, and individualization. Dickinson decides that the most important criterion is the degree of freedom of choice available to the learner. The most useful term is self-directed learning, which implies self-pacing and self-selection of materials and objectives. Within self-directed learning, autonomy represents the greatest degree of freedom. *Individualization*, Dickinson suggests, is not a helpful term, because so many things are meant by it, including a well-established procedure whereby a teacher implementing a teacher or school controlled programme allocates teacher-selected exercises for individual pupils to work through 'on their own'.

Despite Dickinson's clear presentation of the meaning and value of the different terms, his article appears in a volume entitled *Individualization in language learning* (50). This is perhaps appropriate, however, in that some of the articles there and elsewhere, some referring to ESP, describe programmes involving individualized materials and/or self-selection but not necessarily self-direction.

Thus the ELTI activity options, as described in Geddes and McAlpin (248) occur within an otherwise teacher and institution directed programme. The activity options developed because:

> 'We wanted to offer students a chance to select their preferred learning pursuits, freedom to engage in one activity at length or to change activities at will, and opportunities to regroup or to work alone. And we wanted to find a place on the course programme to utilize certain self-access resources that were less appropriate for standard classroom use.'

The options described consist of 'Press', with a wide range of newspapers, journals and magazines being made available for students to read; 'Games', with a wide range of different communication games being made available; 'Listening', involving the equipping of language laboratory booths with a wide range of tapes and accompanying worksheets, answer sheets and transcripts; 'Research', in which material on library and reference skills is made available in a reference room; and different films and video. Students are free to choose activities and to wander from one activity to another or concentrate on one, as they choose. The activity options can be seen as welcome changes of scene and approach for students in an otherwise non-individualized and teacher-directed course.

Other individualized (their term) courses and approaches to individualization are described by Clausing (239), Tuman (260) and Altman (238). Clausing describes the first year German courses at the University of Minnesota, where three modes of instruction are available: 'Regular', where teacher and students meet for five hours a week, using textbook, workbook and audio tapes; 'Media-aided', where the contact hours are three per week, with two further hours of televised instruction and a computer-tutor for homework; 'Individualized', where there are no contact hours, but in which each student is equipped with the textbooks, the workbook and a book setting out the method of an individualized programme. The choice of mode of instruction depends on a student's attitude and learning style. If a student on the individualized programme fails at self-management he is able to return to the regular course. (Compare the CRAPEL programme, as described by Dickinson, where the learner is reportedly unable to return to a more controlled programme from a more autonomous one.)

Tuman notes that there are many interpretations of the term *self-instruction* (although he entitles his article 'A chronicle of individualization'), but proceeds to specify what it means for him. Crucial elements are the specification of needs, 'close description of on-the-job performance' (target performance presumably), immediate feedback, maximum student self-evaluation and maximum student self-management of instruction, including self-pacing. Tuman suggests that self-instruction is essentially 'eclectic as to methodology'.

A similar eclecticism regarding methodology is expressed by Altman (238). For him, too, the formulation of objectives and the development of efficient tests are important components in the establishment of an individualized programme. The two most important characteristics of individualized instruction, however, are the 'new and unconventional role of the teacher' and the systems approach. Altman writes that 'Accommodation of the instruction program to meet individual needs, interests and abilities may take any or all of the following forms: individualization of pacing, individualization of instructional goals, individualization of the mode of learning, individualization of the learner's expectations.' Altman is writing theoretically, however, and does not give examples of actual programmes.

Most practical articles concerning the individualized approach describe only one component of a course or one basic methodology. Thus Disik (245) describes an individualized approach to the teaching of a grammar unit (though note that he refers to *teaching* rather than *learning*). Tirkonnen-Condit (259) introduces individualization to a translation class, and Logan (254) describes the development of conversational skills in an individualized approach. Vocabulary learning is treated by Cowie (240) and by Saragi *et al* (258). Gorosch (249) also seems to be primarily concerned with vocabulary in his 'pilot programme of English instruction in industrial workshops of Swedish vocational schools'. However, although he writes that 'To compensate for the unavailability of trained English teachers, large use is made of semi-autonomized audio-visual methods and of self-instructional and self-correctional learning methods' his account, largely confined to the description of wall charts, labelled in both English and Swedish, and of word-lists, does not make the self-instructional aspect of the course at all obvious.

The most widely used tools for self-instruction must surely be the language laboratory and the private tape/cassette recorder. Farrington and Richardson (246) describe a self-instructional language lab course based on text study (using 'intrinsically interesting authentic texts' to maintain motivation) and other language lab courses for self-study are described in some of the articles in (66), the majority of them occurring in a university context. Abe *et al* (237) also describe self-study work on recorded texts, first giving students training in the exercise types used. The students' work load was discovered to be unduly high, however, since each text (which had to be listened to many times) had only one exercise on it.

Apart from Abe *et al* and Henner-Stanchina, almost all of the courses referred to, whether containing a small or a fairly large individualized component, seem to keep the teacher and the student in fairly close contact. If the teacher is not present in the classroom as a resource-person, at least he/she is somewhere in the same building/institution. An obvious use for an individualized/self-instructional programme, of course, is when learner and teacher are physically separated by considerable distances. This is the situation described by Davies (241), (242) and Gorosch (249) in Sweden.

The programme that Davies outlines combines elements of a traditional correspondence course with some of the methods of the Open University. Important components, however, are the clear delineation of goals and various testing devices, including some self-assessment, together with instructions on the methods of self-study. The courses are reported to be very successful, contributory factors to success being the ingenious ideas for communication, including telephone teaching and the exchange of cassettes. Abe *et al* (237) also mentions that an essential part of the course was the meeting between students and teacher, in order to discuss methods of self-study.

The most minimal kind of self-instruction aid is a key to exercises in a textbook, as is provided by the *English Studies Series*, for example. An improvement on this is the discussion of possible answers and indication as to the relative merit of different answers, eg in Smithies (330). More books could probably be used for self-instruction than are intended to be, eg *English in Focus* – which has a small component of discussion of answers.

An informal report on the ESP situation in Iran in 1971 (filed in British Council ETIC archives) notes that *'self-instructional* materials continues to be the greatest need'. An obvious problem in the implementation of some types of individualized programme (eg activity options) is the collection of a data bank. It takes time and effort to amass a sufficiency of suitable, relevant materials. As Geddes and McAlpin write (248), (activity options) 'are exhausting to organize'.

A more serious constraint on the implementation of an individualized or learner-directed, programme is the attitude of the teaching staff. Clausing (239) suggests that a teacher-training programme is necessary to prepare teachers for their new role as 'managers of learning'. 'Some few never learn to adapt.' Tuman (260) chronicles the development of an 80-hour workshop for the conversion of staff to the ideas and methods of self-instruction. Henner-Stanchina (252) while not suggesting any kind of conversion course advocates a change of name from 'teacher' to 'helper', and describes the nature of the relationship between helper and learner.

An important element of a self-directed course is self-assessment, at all stages of the course. The most thorough survey of self-assessment in foreign language learning is that made by Oskarsson (256). He found that very little research had been done into self-assessment, and that little in Sweden, Israel, Finland, and at CRAPEL. He surveys a range of different practices, including proficiency tests for potential university applicants in Sweden, multiple-choice attainment tests which are marked by both students and teachers, the use of standardized forms and questionnaires, and the use of informal self-assessment in groups and in authentic situations. The standardized forms, which Oskarsson exemplifies, can be used first of all to assess proficiency in the four skills. The learner can be asked to place himself on a ten-point scale for each of the skills, either 'globally' or in relation to a concrete situation. Alternatively the student can place himself on a descriptive rating scale. The student's control of topics and functions, as based on threshold level objectives, can be assessed by means of a standardized form requiring yes/no answers as to whether the student knows a particular set of exponents or not.

Oskarsson acknowledges that there may be both technical and personality difficulties with the use of self-assessment but realizes that the study of self-assessment and its procedures has essentially only just begun.

Actual systems of self-assessment are described by Ferguson (247) for listening comprehension, and by Nord (255) and Green (250) both referring to the self-administration of error analysis as the input to a lesson/period of study. Some coursebooks have the related idea of tests at the beginning and end of units or sections in order for students to assess their knowledge of a point before and after it is taught (eg Howatt et al (432) and Candlin et al (400)). Some course-writers mention the use of questionnaires at the end of courses, primarily as means of course-evaluation, but including some elements of self-assessment, eg Coutts (342) and Coleman (340).

Bibliography

Each item in the bibliography is numbered to ease reference from the text. The numbering is consecutive throughout the bibliography and items are identified in the text mainly by number.

The items in the bibliography are organized into sections, following the organization of the text and also according to the sub-divisions by special subject in the British Council ETIC Information Guide on ESP (item (25) in the bibliography). Each item is placed in the section thought most appropriate to its subject matter, but it is recognized that other groupings of the items would be possible.

Section

		Page
A.	Journals	94
B.	Project and conference reports	95
C.	Collections of papers and articles	96
D.	Articles relating to definitions of ESP	98
E.	Articles relating to a historical study of ESP	98
F.	Books and articles on register analysis	99
G.	Books and articles on discourse analysis and the communicative approach	102
H.	Books and articles on student motivation and the analysis of needs	102
I.	Articles and papers on syllabus design	103
J.	Articles and papers on materials production	105
K.	Articles and papers on methodology	106
L.	Articles on teacher training	106
M.	Articles on testing and evaluation	107
N.	Articles and papers on self-directed learning	107

O. Series of textbooks 108
P. Articles and textbooks by subject matter 110
   P/1 Social Sciences 110
   P/2 Physical Sciences 111
   P/3 Technology 113
   P/4 Medicine 116
   P/5 Commerce 117
   P/6 Study skills 119
   P/7 Other 121

A. Journals

A/1. Journals concerned mainly with ESP/LSP

1. *English for Business* Stockholm. 10 times a year.
2. *ESP in Alexandria Newsletter* Medical Educational Centre, University of Alexandria. Irregular.
3. *ESPMENA Bulletin* English for Special Purposes in the Middle East and North Africa. English Language Servicing Unit, University of Khartoum. 3 times a year.
4. *EST Newsletter* Oregon, University of Oregon Clearing House. Quarterly.
5. *EST/ESP Chile Newsletter* Santiago. Irregular.
6. *Lenguas Para Objectivos Especificos* Universidad Autonoma Metropolitana Xochimilco, Mexico. Irregular.
7. *NC/LT News Sheet* National Centre for Industrial Language Training, Southall. Alternate months.
8. *Petroleum English Bulletin* Akamigas, Indonesia. 2 times a year.
9. *Unesco ALSED-LSP Newsletter* Copenhagen School of Economics. 3 times a year.

A/2 Journals with occasional articles on ESP

10. *Al Manakh* Newsletter of the Language Centre, University of Kuwait. Annual.
11. *Audio-Visual Language Journal* Journal of Applied Linguistics and Language Teaching. Organ of the British Association for Language Teaching. Bangor, Wales. 3 times a year.
12. *Edutec* Mexico. Monthly.
13. *ELI Monthly* University of Petroleum and Minerals, Dhahran, Saudi Arabia. Monthly.
14. *ELT Documents* British Council. Quarterly.

15. *English Teaching Forum* Washington, DC. 4 times a year.
16. *ELTJ: English Language Teaching Journal* Oxford University Press. Quarterly.
17. *IRAL* International Review of Applied Linguistics & Language Teaching. Heidelberg. Quarterly.
18. *IUT Bulletin Pedagogique: Langes Vivants* Institute Universitaire de Technologie, Versailles. 3 times a year.
19. *Language Teaching & Linguistics: Abstracts* Cambridge University Press. Quarterly.
20. *Mélanges Pédagogiques* Centre de Recherche et d'Applications Pedagogiques en Langues, Nancy. Annual.
21. *MALS Journal* Midlands Association for Linguistic Studies. 2 times a year.
22. *RELC Journal* SEAMEO Regional English Language Centre, Singapore. 2 times a year.
23. *SLANT* Second Language Acquisition Notes and Topics. A Newsletter for Researchers. San José State University, California. Quarterly.
24. *System* The International Journal of Educational Technology & Language Learning Systems. Pergamon Press, Oxford. 3 times a year.
25. *TESOL Quarterly* Georgetown University, Washington, DC. 4 times a year.

B. Project and conference reports

26. Argentina. Report on a seminar-workshop on ESP held at Salta, Argentina, 6th–14th January 1976, by J R Ewer. British Council, ETIC archives.
27. Iran. Documents from the 2nd Regional Conference on ESP, Isfahan, Iran, 6th–10th November 1977. British Council, ETIC archives.
28. Iran. Review/report on the 2nd Regional Conference on ESP, Isfahan, 1977, by J N Crofts, *ESPMENA Bulletin* 9, Winter 1977–78.
29. Iraq. Report on the M. A. programme in teaching ESP at Mosul University, Iraq, by P Falvey. British Council, ETIC archives.
30. Iraq. Report on the M A programme in teaching ESP at Mosul University, Iraq. *ESPMENA Bulletin* 11, Autumn 1978.
31. Malaya. Report on the University of Malaya English for Special Purposes Project, given at the 11th SEAMEO RELC Regional Seminar, July 1975, by M D Cooper. British Council, ETIC archives.
32. Malaya. Report on the University of Malaya English for Special Purposes Project, by J McH Sinclair. British Council, ELT Documents 75/3.
33. Philippines. Report on an ESP Seminar in Manila, October 1978, by B Coffey. British Council, ETIC archives.
34. Saudi Arabia. First yearly report on the King Abdul Aziz University

English for Academic Purposes Project, October 1976, by H G Widdowson and A H Urquhart, University of Edinburgh/K A A University.
35. Thailand. Report on a Science and Technology in English workshop at the Central Institute of English Language, Bangkok, 26th May–6th June 1975. British Council, ETIC archives.
36. Thailand. Report on the Special Purpose English Materials Project at the Central Institute of English Language, Bangkok, June–October 1976, by A Bradford. British Council, ETIC archives.
37. Thailand. Report on the English Language Teaching Project in English for Science and Technology at King Mongkut Institute of Technology, September 1976–September 1978. British Council, ETIC archives.
38. Tunisia. Report on a conference on ESP, Hammamet, Tunisia, February 1975. British Council, ETIC archives.
39. United Kingdom. *Survey of research and materials development in vocational uses of English, French and German* 1975. CILT.
40. United Kingdom, Ministry of Overseas Development/British Council *Report of the working group on English for Specific Purposes* 1977. ODM, BC.
41. United Kingdom. Report of the Working Party of the Standing Conference of Heads of Modern Languages in Polytechnics and other Colleges into *Languages for Special Purposes* 1977. SCHML.
42. United Kingdom. Report on the Dunford House Seminar *ESP Course Design* 1978. British Council/ELCD.
43. United States. Report on the 1978 TESOL Convention by K Drobnic and K Michaels *ESPMENA Bulletin* 11, Autumn 1978.

C. Collections of papers and articles

44. British Council, English Teaching Information Centre (1975) *English for Academic Study with special reference to Science and Technology. Problems and perspectives* An ETIC occasional paper. British Council.
45. British Council, English Teaching Information Centre (1976) *English for Specific Purposes: Information Guide no 2* British Council.
46. Review of British Council, ETIC (1976) by Swales, J, in *ESPMENA Bulletin 5*, Autumn 1976.
47. British Council (1977) *English for Specific Purposes: An international seminar.* Proceedings of a seminar held at Bogota, Colombia 17th–22nd April 1977. British Council.
48. British Council, English Teaching Information Centre (1978a) *English for Specific Purposes.* ELT Documents 101. British Council.
49. Review of British Council ETIC (1978a) by Bex, T, in *ESPMENA Bulletin* 11, Autumn 1978.
50. British Council, English Teaching Information Centre (1978b) *Individualization in language learning* ELT Documents 103, British Council.

51. British Council English Teaching Information Centre (1978c) *Pre-sessional courses for overseas students* An ETIC occasional paper. British Council.
52. Cowie, A P, and J B Heaton *(eds)* (1977) *English for Academic Purposes* BAAL/SELMOUS. Centre for Applied Language Studies, University of Reading.
53. Drobnic, K *(ed)* (1978) *38 ESP textbook reviews* EST Clearing House, English Language Institute, Oregon State University, Oregon.
54. de Grève, M, *et al (eds)* (1973) *Modern Language teaching to adults: Language for Special Purposes* 2nd AIMAV Seminar with the collaboration of ASLA Stockholm, 27th–30th April 1972. AIMAV, Brussels; Didier, Paris.
55. Holden, S *(ed)* (1977) *English for Specific Purposes* Modern English Publications.
56. Johnson, K *(ed)* (1977) *SELMOUS Occasional Papers No 1* Centre for Applied Language Studies, University of Reading.
57. Kirkman, J *(ed)* (1978) *Teaching communication skills to engineers and scientists in higher education* Papers from a one day conference at Cardiff, 17th November 1978.
58. Mackay, R *(ed) Review and analysis of thirteen ESP textbooks* EST Clearinghouse, English Language Institute, Oregon State University.
59. Mackay, R, and A Mountford *(eds)* (1978) *English for Specific Purposes* Longman.
60. Review of Mackay R, and A Mountford *(eds)* (1978) by T Bex, in *ESPMENA Bulletin* 11, Autumn 1978.
61. Review of Mackay, R, and A Mountford *(eds)* (1978) by R Turner in *ALSED-LSP Newsletter* 2, 2(5) October 1978.
62. Review of Mackay, R, and A Mountford *(eds)* (1978) by C Nuttall in *BAAL Newsletter* (British Association for Applied Linguistics), no 6, March 1979.
63. *1st National Seminar on Vocational English* (1978) Department of Languages, State Technical University, Santiago, Chile, March 1978.
64. Perren, G *(ed)* (1969) *Languages for Special Purposes* (CILT Reports and Papers No 1) CILT.
65. Perren, G *(ed)* (1971) *Science and Technology in a second language* (CILT Reports and Papers No 7) CILT.
66. Perren, G *(ed)* (1974) *Teaching languages to adults for Special Purposes* (CILT Reports and Papers No 11) CILT.
67. Richards, J *(ed)* (1976) *Teaching English for Science and Technology* Selected papers from the RELC Seminar on the teaching and learning of English for Scientific and Technological Purposes in Southeast Asia, Singapore. 21st–25th April 1975. Singapore University Press.
68. Selinker, L, L Trimble, and R Vroman (1972) *Working Papers in English for Science and Technology* University of Washington, Seattle.

69. Trimble, Louis, Mary Todd Trimble and Karl Drobnic (*eds*) (1978) *English for Specific Purposes: Science and Technology* English Language Institute, Oregon State University.

D. Articles relating to definitions of ESP

70. Brumfit, C (1977) 'Commonsense about ESP', in Holden (*ed*) (55), reproduced in *Problems and principles in English teaching* Pergamon Press, Oxford, 1979.
71. Fitzjohn, B (1974) 'Problems of organization', in Perren (*ed*) (66).
72. Lilley, A D (1976) 'A rationale for an ESP approach to teaching English to students of economics at the University of Benghazi, Libya' British Council, ETIC archives.
73. Mackay, R (1975) 'Languages for Special Purposes' *Edutec* 3, April 1975.
74. Mackay, R, and A Mountford (1978) 'The teaching of English for Special Purposes: theory and practice', in Mackay and Mountford (*eds*) (59).
75. Pritchard, N A, and R G G Chamberlain (1974) 'Special Purpose English: changing approaches to English language teaching' *RELC Journal* 5, 2, December 1974.
76. Sager, J C, and D Dungworth (1978) 'The nature and function of special subject languages' *Incorporated Linguist* 17, 3, 1978.
77. Sinclair, J (1975) 'English for Special Purposes' Paper given at the Ford Foundation Conference in Hammamet, Tunisia. British Council, ELT Documents 76/3.
78. Spencer, J (1973) 'Languages for Special Purposes: teaching rules or learning roles?', in de Grève *et al* (54).
79. Strevens, P (1973) 'Technical, technological and scientific English' *ELT Journal* 27, 3, June 1973.
80. Strevens, P (1977a) 'ESP: an analysis and a survey' *Studies in Language Learning* 2, 1, 1977.
81. Strevens, P (1977b) 'Special-purpose language learning: a perspective', Survey article. *Language Teaching & Linguistics: Abstracts* 10, 3, July 1977.
82. Strevens, P (1977c) 'The Teaching of English for Special Purposes', in Strevens, P *New orientations in the teaching of English* Oxford University Press.
83. Trim, J L M (1976) 'Languages for adult learners' Survey article. *Language Teaching & Linguistics: Abstracts* 9, 2, April 1976.
84. Widdowson, H G (1979a) 'EST in theory and practice', in British Council (1975) (44).

E. Articles relating to a historical study of ESP

85. Corbluth, J D (1975) 'English or Special English?' *ELT Journal* 29, 4.

86. Lee Kok Cheong (1976) 'Trends in the linguistic study of EST', in Richards *(ed)* (67).
87. Tickoo, M L (1976) 'Theories and materials in EST· a view from Hyderabad', in Richards *(ed)* (67).

F. Books and articles on register analysis

88. Anthony, EM (1976) 'English for Special Purposes: a lexical content', in Richards *(ed)* (67).
89. Barber, C (1962) 'Some measurable characteristics of modern scientific prose', in *Contributions to English Syntax and Philology* Stockholm. Also in British Council, ETIC archives.
90. Bares, K (1969) Semantic features of quantitative prefixes in technical English *Philologica Pragensia* 12, 3.
91. Bares, K (1972) 'The morphological features of technical English and their presentation in teaching', in Fried, V *(ed) The Prague School of Linguistics and Language Teaching* Oxford University Press.
92. Bartolic, L (1978) 'Nominal compounds in technical English', in Todd Trimble, Trimble and Drobnic *(eds)* (69).
93. Behan, N (1976) Notes of word-formation in scientific and technical English *English Teaching Forum* 14, 1, January 1976.
94. Byrd, P (1978) 'English linguistics and the English of science and technology', in Todd Trimble, Trimble and Drobnic *(eds)* (69).
95. Chiu, R (1972) 'Register constraints on the choice of the English verb' Paper given at the 1972 TESOL Convention.
96. Cooper, M D (1974) 'Language roles in the study of Science' British Council, *ELT Documents* 74/2.
97. Douglas, D (1976) What is scientific vocabulary? *ESPMENA Bulletin* 5, Autumn 1976.
98. Ewer, J R, and E Hughes-Davies (1974) 'Instructional English' British Council, *ELT Documents* 74/4.
99. Friel, M (1978) A verb frequency count in legal English *ESPMENA Bulletin* 10, Spring 1978.
100. Garwood, G H (1972) Register and style in the teaching of English for Special Purposes *IUT Bulletin Pédagogique* 18, February 1972.
101. Godman, A (1976 'The language of science from the viewpoint of the writer of Science books' Paper given at the CIEL Seminar, 1976. British Council, ETIC archives, 959 Thailand.
102. Gopnik, M (1972) *Linguistic structures in scientific texts* The Hague, Mouton.
103. Gustaffson, M (1975) *Some syntactic properties of English law language* University of Turku, Finland.
104. Huddleston, R D, *et al* (1968) *Sentence and clause in scientific English*

Communication Research Centre, Department of General Linguistics, University College, London.
105. Huddleston, R D (1971) *The sentence in written English: a syntactic study based on an analysis of written texts* Cambridge University Press.
106. Review of Huddleston, R D (1971) by J Swales in *ESPMENA Bulletin* 3, Winter 1975–76.
107. Hughes, M N (1974) Introduction to a paper on the language of administration and public relations. British Council, ETIC archives.
108. Inman, M (1978) 'Lexical analysis of scientific and technical prose', in Todd Trimble, Trimble and Drobnic (*eds*) (69).
109. Kirkman, J (1978) How common are 'common core' words? *ESPMENA Bulletin* 10, Spring 1978.
110. Lackstrom, J E, L Selinker, and L Trimble (1972) Grammar and technical English *English Teaching Forum* 10, 5.
111. Lackstrom, J E, L Selinker, and L Trimble (1973) Technical rhetorical principles and grammatical choice *English Teaching Forum* 11, 3 (also in *TESOL Quarterly* 7, 2)
112. Mellinkoff, D (1963) *The Language of the Law* Little, Brown & Co, Boston.
113. Meredith, P (1966) *Instruments of communication: an essay on scientific writing* Pergamon Press, Oxford.
114. Owens, G T (1970) *English words and structures in Science and Maths* Teachers Training College, Singapore.
115. Porter, D (1976) Scientific English: an oversight in stylistics? *Studia Anglica Posnaniensia* 8, Poznan.
116. Puangmali, S (1976) A study of engineering English vocabulary *RELC Journal* 7, 1, June 1976.
117. Rumszewicz, W (1967) On contemporary dramatic and scientific English *Glottodidactica* 2, Poznan.
118. Sarma, G V L N (1966) A list of professional words commonly used in technology and engineering *Teaching English* IX, 1, April 1966.
119. Sastri, M I (1968) Prepositions in chemical abstracts *Linguistics* 38.
120. Savory, T H (1953) *The language of Science: its growth, character and use* Andre Deutsch.
121. Sears, D A (1971) The noun adjuncts of modern English *Linguistics* 72.
122. Selinker, L, L Trimble, and R Vroman (1974) Presupposition and technical rhetoric *ELT Journal* 29, 1.
123. Selinker, L, R M Todd Trimble, and L Trimble (1976) 'On reading EST: presuppositional rhetorical information in the discourse', in Richards (*ed*) (67).
124. Selinker, L, R M Todd Trimble, and L Trimble (1976) Presuppositional rhetorical information in EST discourse *TESOL Quarterly* 10, 3.
125. Selinker, L, and L Trimble (1976) Scientific and technical writing: the choice of tense. *English Teaching Forum* 14, 4.

126. Selinker, L, *et al* (1978) Rhetorical function shifts in EST discourse *TESOL Quarterly* 12, 3.
127. Spathaky, R (1970) The international scientific vocabulary and the new international languages *Linguistics* 61.
128. Spencer, A (1975a) *Noun-verb expressions in legal English, a handbook for speakers of Arabic* English Language Servicing Unit and the Faculty of Law, University of Khartoum.
129. Spencer, A (1975b) Semantic combinations in Economics and law – a case for special treatment *ESPMENA Bulletin* 3, Winter 1975–76.
130. Strevens, P (1977c) 'Varieties of English: the description of diversity', in Strevens, P *New orientations in the teaching of English* Oxford University Press.
131. Strevens, P (1977) 'Varieties of English: a TEFL approach', in Strevens, P *New orientations in the teaching of English* Oxford University Press.
132. Swales, J (1974) 'Notes on the function of attributive -en participles in scientific discourse', in *Papers in English for Special University Purpose, 1* University of Khartoum Press.
133. Swales, J (1976) Latinate names and article usage in Biology *ESPMENA Bulletin* 6, Winter 1976–77.
134. Tan San Yee, C (1979) Sequence signals in technical English *RELC Journal* 6, 2.
135. Thakur, D (1969) *A stylistic description of four restricted uses of English in Science* PhD thesis, University of Reading.
136. Tinkler, T C (1978) *The use of the passive in certain Social Science lectures, and implications for teaching English to non-native speakers* MEd thesis, University of Manchester.
137. Todd Trimble, R M, and L Trimble (1977) Literary training and the teaching of scientific and technical English *English Teaching Forum* 15, 2, April 1977.
138. Trimble, L An approach to reading scientific and technical English *Lenguas Para Objectivos Especificos* Cuaderno 4 (undated).
139. White, R V (1974) Communicative competence, register and second language learning *IRAL* XII, 2.
140. White, R V (1975) The language, the learner and the syllabus *RELC Journal* 6, 1, June 1975.
141. Widdowson, H G (1974) Literary and scientific uses of English *ELT Journal* 28, 4.
142. Wingard, P, and L Thompson (1976) Some verb forms and functions in some medical texts *ESPMENA Bulletin* 6, Winter 1976–77.
143. Winter, E O (1971) 'Connection in science material', in Perren (*ed*) (65).

G. Books and articles on discourse analysis and the communicative approach

144. Allen, J P B, and H G Widdowson (1974) Teaching the communicative use of English *IRAL* 12, 1 (also in Mackay and Mountford (*eds*) (*59*).
145. Candlin, C (1973) 'The communicative teaching of English' British Council, *ELT Documents* 73/4.
146. Johns, T (1975) *The application of the theory of discourse analysis to the production of materials for English for academic purposes* Paper given at the 10th Regional RELC Seminar, Singavore, 1975.
147. Jones, K (1974) 'The role of discourse analysis in devising undergraduate reading programmes in EST' British Council, ETIC archives.
148. Sim, D D (1974) *Grammatical cohesion in English and advanced reading comprehension for overseas students* MEd thesis, University of Manchester.
149. Urquhart, A H (1976) *The effect of rhetorical organization on the readability of study texts.* PhD thesis, University of Edinburgh.
150. Widdowson, H G (1972) The teaching of English as communication *ELT Journal* 27, 1.
151. Widdowson, H G (1974) An approach to the teaching of scientific English discourse *RELC Journal* 5, 1.
152. Widdowson, H G (1975) *Stylistics and the teaching of literature* Longman.
153. Widdowson, H G (1977) 'The communicative approach and its application', in British Council (1977) (*47*).
154. Widdowson, H G (1978) *Teaching language as communication* Oxford University Press.

H. Books and articles on student motivation and the analysis of needs

155. Campbell, V (1974) *The communications problems of overseas students in British technical education* NE London Polytechnic.
156. Davis, R (1977) 'All protein and no roughage makes Hamid a constipated student', in Holden (*ed*) (*55*).
157. Emmans, K, E Hawkins, and A Westoby (1976) *Foreign languages in industry and commerce* Language Teaching Centre, University of York, reviewed in *Audio-Visual Language Journal* 14, 1, Spring 1976.
158. Emmans, K (1978) 'The subsequent use of French and German in employment and leisure by "A" level candidates' Project reported in *Language Teaching & Linguistics: Abstracts* 11, 2, April, 1978.
159. Gorosch, M (1976) Modern language teaching to adults for professional use *ALSED-LSP Newsletter* 5, June 1976.

160. James, C V, and S Rouve (1973) *Survey of curricula and performance in modern languages 1971–1972* CILT.
161. Lee, E V (1977) Non-specialist of foreign languages in industry and commerce *Audio-Visual Language Journal* 15, 3. Winter 1977–78.
162. McDonald, P F, and J C Sager (1975) Beyond contextual studies *IRAL* 13, 1, February 1975.
163. Mackay, R (1978) 'Identifying the nature of the learner's needs', in Mackay and Mountford (*eds*) (59).
164. Moody, K W *A report on responses to a RELC questionnaire* British Council, ETIC archives, 959, SE Asia.
165. Moulin, A (1975) Foreign languages for non-linguists: assessing the needs and defining the teaching approaches *System* 3, 2.
166. Munby, J L (1977) 'Processing profiles of communicative needs', in British Council (1977) (47).
167. Munby, J L (1978) *Communicative syllabus design* Cambridge University Press.
168. Review of Munby, J L (1978) by C Brumfit, in *Times Educational Supplement* 11th August 1978.
169. O'Neill, R (1977) 'The limits of functional/notional syllabuses' – or 'My guinea pig died with its legs crossed', in Holden (*ed*) (55).
170. Van-Passel, F (1973) 'Sense and nonsense in defining ELT objectives', in de Grève *et al* (*eds*) (54).
171. Payne, R M (1975) Who says what? The rationale for language surveys in preparing language materials for Special Purposes *Edutec* 9, November 1975.
172. Richterich, R, and J L Chancerel (1978) *Identifying the needs of adults learning a foreign language* Council for Cultural Cooperation of the Council of Europe, Strasbourg.
173. Schroeder, K (1973) 'Theses on European language politics and ensuing curricular decisions in the field of adult language education', in de Grève *et al* (*eds*) (54).
174. Stevenson, J L (1977) Student attitudes towards language, learning, and language learning *System* 5, 3, October 1977.

I. Articles and papers on syllabus design

175. Alderson *et al* (1978) 'A framework for the production of an ESP course', presented at the 5th AILA Conference, Montreal, August 1978. Reported in *ESPMENA Bulletin* 11, Autumn 1978.
176. Blackie, D J J S (1976) 'Service English' for students of Science and Technology *English Teaching Forum* 14, 2, April 1976.
177. Drobnic, K (1978) 'Mistakes and modifications in course design: an EST case history', in Todd Trimble, Trimble and Drobnic (*eds*) (69).

178. Gerighty, T A (1976) What to do about 'Special English' *English Teaching Forum* 14, 1, January 1976.
179. Harvey, A, and G Sindermann 'The design of an ESP course. An account of practical experience' British Council, ETIC archives, Chile, 983. Also in *EST/ESP Chile Newsletter* no 3.
180. Hirayama-Grant, G, and M Sedgwick (1978) ESP syllabus design processes in retrospect in Todd Trimble, Trimble and Drobnic (*eds*) (69).
181. Hughes-Davies, E (1975) The organization and administration of an EST programme' Paper given at the CIEL Seminar and workshop on EST, Thailand, 1975. British Council, ETIC archives, 959, Thailand.
182. Jones, K, and P Roe (1975) Designing English for Science and Technology programmes in British Council (1975) (44). Also appears as 'Problems in designing programmes in English for Science and Technology', in Richards (*ed*) (67).
183. Opitz, K (1973) 'Factor control as a strategy in second and third-language teaching', in de Grève *et al* (*eds*) (54).
184. Perry, F A (1976) The systems approach to basic English language training in the Canadian armed forces *System* 4, 3, October 1976.
185. Phillips, M, and C Shettlesworth (1975a) Problems in syllabus design for a course in industrial English *ESPMENA Bulletin* 2, Autumn 1975.
186. Phillips, M, and C Shettlesworth (1975b) Questions in the design and use of courses in English for specialized purposes. *Proceedings of the 4th International Conference of Applied Linguists* Stuttgart, 1975 (Nickel, G (*ed*)).
187. Pittman, G A (1974) A suggested strategy for 'vocational' courses in English for adults *ELT Journal* 28, 2, January 1974.
188. Sager, J C (1978) LSP – Projects on a large scale *ALSED-LSP Newsletter* 2, 1(4) July 1978.
189. Sandulescu, C G (1973) 'LTA and LSP: Towards a semiotic-sociolinguistic approach', in de Grève *et al* (*eds*) (54).
190. Sculthorp, M A L (1974) 'Intensive courses: towards a strategy for teaching', in Perren, G (*ed*) (66).
191. Shaw, A M (1977) 'Foreign-language syllabus development: some recent approaches' Survey article. *Language Teaching & Linguistics: Abstracts* 10, 4, October 1977.
192. Sitachitta, K, and P Sagarik (1976) 'Problems and attempts at solutions in the teaching of ESP at the tertiary level in Thailand', in Richards (*ed*) (67).
193. Smithies, M (1976) 'Weighting the four skills in tertiary EST programme', in Richards (*ed*) (67).
194. Tan San Yee, C (1975) 'A proposed technical English syllabus for 1st year engineering students at Ngei Ann Technical College, Singapore' British Council, ETIC archives, 959, SE Asia.

195. Trim, J M L (1969) 'Linguistic considerations in the planning of language courses for Special Purposes', in Perren (ed) (1969) (64).
196. Webb, J (1977) Reflections of practical experience in designing and mounting ESP courses at the Colchester English Study Centre *IUT Bulletin Pedagogique* May 1977.

J. Articles and papers on materials production

197. Abbott, G (1978) 'Motivation, materials, manpower and methods: some fundamental problems in ESP', in British Council (1978b) (50).
198. Bates, M (1978) 'Writing *Nucleus*', in Mackay and Mountford (eds) (59).
199. Bruton, J G (1961) The simplification of technical literature *ELT Journal* 16, 1.
200. Cobb, D (1972) Aural comprehension materials for tertiary level Science and Technical students *RELC Journal* 3, 1 and 2, June–December 1972.
201. Dudley-Evans, A, C C Shettlesworth and M K Phillips (1976) 'The ESP materials of the University of Azarabadegan, Tabriz, Iran', in Richards (ed) (67).
202. Ewer J R, and G Latorre (1967) Preparing an English course for students of Science *ELT Journal* 21, 3, May 1967.
203. Fox, J (1978) TELEFUN: A pragmatic approach to functional learning materials development *TESOL Quarterly* 12, 3, September 1978.
204. Harvey, A M, M Horzella, and G Latorre (1977) 'Materials production for ESP – some first principles', in British Council (1977) (47).
205. Mackay, R (1973) ESP: English and the environment *IUT Bulletin Pedagogique* 24.
206. Moore, J D (1977 'The preparation of rhetorically focused materials for service courses in English', in British Council (1977) (47).
207. Morrow K (1977) 'Authentic texts and ESP', in Holden (ed) (55).
208. Phillips, M K, and C C Shettlesworth (1978) 'How to ARM your students: a consideration of two approaches to providing materials for ESP', in British Council (1978a) (48).
209. Smithies, M (1972) A varied approach to a writing course in English *RELC Journal* 2, 2.
210. Tadros, A A (1977) Principles underlying materials preparation for students of economic and social studies *ESPMENA Bulletin* 8, Autumn 1977.
211. Todd Trimble, R M, and L Trimble (1977) 'The development of EFL materials for occupational English', in British Council (1977) (47).
212. Widdowson, H G (1976) 'The authenticity of language data', in Fanselow, J F, and R H Grymes (eds) *on TESOL '76* TESOL, Washington, DC.

K. Articles and papers on methodology

213. Ewer, J R (1974) 'Catenized vocabulary units' Abstract from a seminar on EST University of Chile, Santiago. British Council, ETIC archives.
214. Hansen, I G (1978) LSP – Aspects of teaching methods at university level *ALSED-LSP Newsletter* 2, 1(4) July 1978.
215. Hara, M (1978) 'Developing skills for reading technical manuals', in Todd Trimble, Trimble and Drobnic (*eds*) (69).
216. Hartman, R R K (1976) Understanding texts *Systems* 3, 2.
217. Hesketh, P M (1974) 'An RAF view of language learning', in Perren (*ed*) (1974) (66).
218. Hilton, M (1970) Audio-visual aids and language laboratory exercises for students with specialist needs *IUT Bulletin Pedagogique* 9, November 1970.
219. Hughes, G, and M Knight (1977) 'Student specific English – one-to-one courses', in Holden (*ed*) (55).
220. Lee, D A (1969) The language laboratory and reading in a foreign language *Audio-Visual Language Journal* 7, 2, Summer 1969.
221. Mackay, R, B Klassen, and T Garst (1975) Practical steps towards the classification of reading – comprehension exercise types *Edutec* 6, July 1979.
222. Mackay, R, and A Mountford (1976) Pedagogic alternatives to 'explication de texte' with special reference to English for Science and Technology *IUT Bulletin Pedagogique* 44, October 1976.
223. Mountford, A (1976) 'The notion of simplification: its relevance to materials preparation for English for Science and Technology', in Richards (*ed*) (67).
224. Sopher, E (1974) An introductory approach to the teaching of scientific English to foreign students *ELT Journal* 28, 4, July 1974.
225. Stanley, J (1975) *Towards a theory of teaching English for special purposes including units of practical work* MA thesis, University of Lancaster.
226. Swales, J (1970) Language laboratory materials and service courses: problems of tape course design for Science students *Audio-visual Language Journal* 8, 1, Spring 1970.

L. Articles on teacher training

227. Ewer, J R (1974a) 'Preparing the budget for a STTE programme' British Council, ETIC archives 983.
228. Ewer, J R (1976a) 'Idea following exercises' British Council, ETIC archives 983
229. Ewer, J R (1976b) 'Teacher training for Science and Technology: the

specialized training of teachers and programme organizers', in Richards (*ed*) (67).
230. Jupp, T C (1977) 'Developing skills and resources for teachers in an ESP situation', in British Council (1977) (47).
231. Swales, J (1975) Introducing teachers to EST *Edutec* 3, April 1975.
232. Swales, J (1978) 'ESP in the Middle East', in Holden (*ed*) (55).

M. Articles on testing and evaluation

233. Davies, N F (1973) A testing and feedback project using a desk computer *System* 1, 2.
234. ELTDU (1976) *Stages of attainment scale and test battery* ELTDU/OUP in collaboration with SKF, Sweden.
235. Ewer, J R (1974b) 'Evaluation in STTE programmes' British Council, ETIC archives 983.
236. Vance, S (1978) 'A placement test for an English for Science programme', in Holden (*ed*) (55).

N. Articles and papers on self-directed learning

237. Abe, D, C Henner-Stanchina, and P Smith (1975) New approaches to autonomy: two experiments in self-directed learning *Mélanges Pédagogiques* CRAPEL.
238. Altman, H B (1977) Individualized foreign language instruction and systems thinking: symbiosis and synergism *System* 5, 2, May 1977.
239. Clausing, G (1975) The individualized dimension and media-aided language programs *System* 3, 1, January 1975.
240. Cowie, A P (1978) 'Vocabulary exercises within an individualized study programme', in British Council (1978b) (50).
241. Davies, N F (1977a) The changing role of the university language department *System* 5, 1, January 1977.
242. Davies, N F (1977b) Language teaching at a distance, a challenge to the university department *IRAL* 15, 3, August 1977.
243. Dickinson, L (1974) 'A student centred approach to language lab methodology' British Council, ETIC archives.
244. Dickinson, L (1978) 'Autonomy, self-directed learning and individualization', in British Council (1978b) (50).
245. Disick, R S (1977) A system for flexible pacing within a 'lockstep' foreign language programme *System* 5, 2, May 1977.
246. Farrington, B, and C Richardson (1977) A self instructional language laboratory course in French for first year university students *Audio-Visual Language Journal* 15, 3, Winter 1977-78.
247. Ferguson, N (1978) Self-assessment of listening comprehension *IRAL* 16, 2.

248. Geddes, M, and J McAlpin (1978) 'Activity options in language courses', in British Council (1978b) (50).
249. Gorosch, M (1967) Teaching by telephone: an experiment in language teaching *IRAL* 5, 2.
250. Green, J (1978) 'English for overseas students', in British Council (1978b) (50).
251. Grittner, F M (1977) Democratization of the foreign language program through individualized instruction *System* 5, 2, May 1977.
252. Henner-Stanchina, C (1975) Autonomous learning as a strategy for adult education. An interim report on an experimental scheme *IUT Bulletin Pédagogique* 38, June 1975.
253. Higgens, J C, and J E Davis (1978) 'Towards individualization: organizing learning in an institutionalized setting', in British Council (1978b) (50).
254. Logan, G E (1977) Developing conversational skills in individualized foreign language programs: a systematic approach *System* 5, 2, May 1977.
255. Nord, J R (1977) Error recognition as a self-monitoring skill *System* 5, 3, October 1977.
256. Oskarsson, M (1978) *Approaches to self-assessment in foreign language learning* Council for Cultural Cooperation of the Council of Europe, Strasbourg.
257. Ross, L (1975) Self-instructional language laboratory reading courses based on auditory perception *System* 3, 2, May 1975.
258. Saragi, T, I S P Nation, and G F Meister (1978) Vocabulary learning and reading *System* 6, 2, May 1978.
259. Tirkonnen-Condit, S (1978) Individualization for a translation class *System* 6, 3, October 1978.
260. Tuman, W V (1978) A chronicle of individualization *System* 6, 1, January 1978.

O. Series of textbooks

261. *English for Careers Series* Regents Publishing Company, New York.
A large series, mainly on the technical side, including *The language of tourism*, *Air travel*, *The merchant marine*, *The petroleum industry*, *Accounting*, *Money*, *Banking*. Emphasis: vocabulary. Textbook only.
262. *English in Focus* Oxford University Press.
Emphasis: reading and writing for the student in higher education. Student's book, teacher's book, taped material. Titles so far are:
 English in Physical Science Allen, J P B, and H G Widdowson
 English in Mechanical Engineering Glendinning, E
 English in workshop practice Mountford, A
 English in basic Medical Science Maclean, J

English in Agriculture Mountford, A
English in Education Laird, E
English in Social Studies Allen, J P B, and H G Widdowson
English in Biological Science Pearson, I

263. *English for Special Purposes Series* Evans Brothers.
A new series by Nicolas Ferguson and Maire O'Reilly, all with accompanying cassettes. Titles so far are:
English Telephone Conversations
English for Bank Cashiers
English for Hotel Staff
English for Banking
Listening and Note-taking
Reading Scientific Texts

264. *English Studies Series* Oxford University Press
Each book contains 20–30 extracts from authentic texts, followed by comprehension and language exercises. The following subject areas are covered:
   1. History, Sociology, Politics, Economics, Law. Clarke, M J
   2. Anthropology, Psychology, Education, Language, Philosophy. Clarke, M J
   3. Physics, Mathematics, Biology and Applied Science. Hawkins, W F, and Mackin, R
   4. Liberal Studies. Mackin, R, and W F Hawkins.
   5. Military Texts. Graver, B D, and K J T Hoile
   6. Zoology and Botany. Gethin, R H, and Mackin, R
   7. Chemistry. Hawkins, W F, R Mackin, and G V Taylor
   8. Language Teaching Texts. Widdowson, H G
   9. General Engineering Texts. Adamson, V, and M J B Lowe
   10. Agriculture. Berkoff, N A
   11. Geography. Biddulph, G M R

265. *Nucleus – English for Science and Technology* Longman.
A core book, *General Science*, and related books for different subjects, aimed at beginning students in higher education. Each book is accompanied by Teacher's Notes and cassette material. Titles so far include:
General Science Bates, M, and T Dudley-Evans
Biology Bates, M, and D Adamson
Agriculture Shettlesworth, C, L Kerr, N S Denny, and M Philips
Engineering Dudley-Evans, T, J Wall, and J Smart
Chemistry Hatward, T, C Barron, and I Stewart
Geology Barron, C, and I Stewart
Mathematics Bowyer, T, and D Hall
Medicine Jameson, J, and D Kirwan
Nursing Science Kerr, R, and J Smith

266. *Special English Series* Collier-Macmillan.

Emphasis: vocabulary of a trade or profession. Topics include *Accounting, Advertising, Air travel, Computer programming, The department store, The jet engine, Legal problems, The motor car, Nursing, Seafaring.*

P. Articles and textbooks by subject matter

P/1 Social Sciences

Articles
267. CILT (1974) 'A modern Chinese course', in Perren (*ed*) (1974) (66).
268. Davies, N F (1975) International Economics – a degree course integrating language and business studies *System* 3, 2.
269. Hughes, M N (1974) 'Language teaching in the European Community institutions', in Perren (*ed*) (1974) (66).
270. Jelinek, J (1974) 'Japanese – the integrated dictionary search method', in Perren (*ed*) (1974) (66).
271. Lafuente, R A (1977) Vocabulary on tourism *English Language Journal* 8, 1, March 1977. Buenos Aires.
272. Mead R, and A D Lilley (1975) The use of visual material in teaching English to Economics students *ELT Journal* 29, 2.
273. Neymann, Monika (1978) Information on the study of the language of Economics *ALSED-LSP Newsletter* 2, 1(4), July 1978.
274. Paneth, Eva (1973) 'Service German', in de Grève *et al* (*eds*) (54).
275. Smith, R E F (1974) 'Russian for social scientists', in Perren (*ed*) (1974) (66).
276. Swales, J (1978) The case of cases and other aspects of English for academic legal purposes *IRAL* (forthcoming).

Textbooks
277. Allen, J P B, and H G Widdowson (1978/79) *English in Social Studies* (English in Focus Series) Oxford University Press.
278. van Dijk, T, and A M L de Saegher (1974) *From the Press* Mary Glasgow Publications.
279. English Language Teaching Development Unit (1978) *Assignment Mornesia* Oxford University Press.
280. Laird, Elizabeth (1978) *English in Education* (English in Focus Series) Oxford University Press.
281. McArthur, Tom (1973) *A rapid course in English for students of Economics* Oxford University Press.
282. Review of McArthur, T (1973) by Gillian Hashim *ESPMENA Bulletin* 2 Autumn 1975.
283. McDonald, Peter, and J C Sager (1974) *The languages of English journalism. A workbook for students* Max Hueber Verlag, Munich.
284. Schmitz, Albert (1973) *A look at the Press* Max Hueber Verlag, Munich.

P/2 Physical Sciences

Articles

285. Allen, J P B (1975) English, Science and language teaching: the Focus approach *Edutec* 9.
286. Butler, C S (1974) 'German for Chemists', in Perren *(ed)* (1974) (66).
287. Byrd, Patricia (1977) Chemistry and agentless passive sentences: an ESL:EST exercise *TESOL Newsletter* 11, 5, November 1977.
288. Castanos, F The discourse of Science and teaching ESP at the elementary level *Lenguas para Objectivos Específicos* Cuaderno 4 (undated).
289. Cleary, J (1975) Science teaching in a second language situation *ELT Documents* 75/2. British Council.
290. Cowie A P, and J B Heaton (1977) 'Preparing a writing programme for students of Science and Technology', in Cowie and Heaton *(eds)* (52).
291. Ewer, J R (1977) 'Preparing speed-reading materials for EST' British Council, ETIC archives, 983.
292. Ewer, J R, and E Hughes-Davies (1971) Further notes on developing an ELT programme for students of Science and Technology *ELT Journal* 26, 1.
293. Ewer, J R, and G Latorre (1967) Preparing an English course for students of Science *ELT Journal* 21, 3.
294. Farrokhpey, S (1970) Scientific English for Iranian students *English Teaching Forum* 8, 6, November–December 1970.
295. Godman, Arthur (1976a) 'The language of Science from viewpoint of the writer of Science textbooks', in Richards *(ed)* (67).
296. Godman, Arthur (1976b) Some aspects of teaching English for Science *ELI Monthly* 15, December 1976.
297. Higgins, J J (1966) Hard facts: notes on teaching English to Science students *ELT Journal* 21, 1.
298. McCrae, E (1975) An approach to the teaching of scientific English *Mélanges Pédagogiques* CRAPEL.
299. Macmillan, M (1971) 'Teaching English to scientists of other languages, sense or sensibility?', in Perren *(ed)* (1971) (65).
300. Owen, G T (1975) A reading comprehension course for students of Science and Technology *Edutec* 3, April 1975.
301. Newberry, R C (1974) English language support for the teaching of Maths and Science in Singaporean primary schools *ELT Documents* 74/4. British Council.
302. Read, M, and H Wainman (1977) 'Language competence in Mathematics' British Council, ETIC archives.
303. Strevens, P (1971) 'Alternatives to daffodils – or scientist thou never wert', in Perren *(ed)* (1971) (65).

304. Swales, John (1978) 'Writing scientific English', in Mackay, R, and A Mountford (eds) (1978) (59).
305. Weissberg, R, and S Buker (1978) Strategies for teaching the rhetorics of written English for Science and Technology *TESOL Quarterly* 12, 3, September 1978.
306. Widdowson, H G (1968) 'The teaching of English through Science', in Dakin, J *et al* (1968). *Language in Education* Oxford University Press.
307. Widdowson, H G (1971) 'The teaching of rhetoric to students of Science and Technology', in Perren (*ed*) (1971) (65).
308. Wilardjo, Liek (1976) 'Reflections of a scientist on teaching the English of Science', in Richards (*ed*) (67).
309. Wood, I N (1967) The foreign language problems facing scientists and technologists in the UK. Report of a recent survey. *Journal of Documentation* 23, 2.

Textbooks

310. Allen, J P B, and H G Widdowson (1974) *English in Physical Science* (English in Focus Series) Oxford University Press.
311. Review of Allen and Widdowson (1974) in *ESPMENA Bulletin* 4, 1976.
312. Review of Allen and Widdowson (1974) by M Tay, in *RELC Journal* 7, 1, 1976.
313. Blackie, David (1978) *English for basic Maths* Nelson.
314. Bolitho, A R, and P L Sandler (1977) *Learn English for Science* Longman.
315. Review of Bolitho and Sandler (1977) by K Drobnic, in *TESOL Quarterly* 12, 2, 1978.
316. BBC (1967) *The scientist speaks. The English for Science and Technology* BBC Publications.
317. BBC (1971) *Scientifically speaking* BBC Publications.
318. Brooks, H F, and H Ross (1967) *English as a foreign language for Science students* Heinemann.
319. Close, R A (1965) *The English we use for Science* Longman.
320. Croft, K, and B W Brown (1965) *Science readings for students of English as a Second Language* McGraw-Hill.
321. English Language Teaching Development Unit (1974) *Basic English for Science* Oxford University Press.
322. Ewer, J R, and G Latorre (1969) *A course in basic scientific English* Longman.
323. Review of Ewer and Latorre (1969) by B A Becker, in *TESOL Quarterly* 7, 2, 1973.
324. Ferguson, N, and M O'Reilly (forthcoming) *Reading scientific texts* Evans.
325. Lucas, D J, H I James, and O J Simpson (1976) *A first Science dictionary* Nelson.

326. Pearson, I (1978) *English in Biological Science* (English in Focus Series) Oxford University Press.
327. Price, R F (1966) *A reference book for foreign Science students* Pergamon Press, Oxford.
328. Royds-Irmak D E (1975) *Beginning scientific English* Nelson.
329. Review of Royds-Irmak (1975) in *ESPMENA Bulletin* 2, 1975.
330. Smithies, M (1972) *Advanced comprehension texts for Science students* Collier-Macmillan.
331. Review of Smithies, M (1972) by P Skeldon, in *ESPMENA Bulletin* 3, Winter 1975–76.
332. Thornley, G C (1972) *Scientific English practice* Longman.
333. Sturgess, P W (1975) *The English for Mathematics* The Green Mountain Press.
334. Swales, John (1971) *Writing scientific English* Nelson.
335. Review of Swales, J (1971) by J Hafseth, in *ELI Monthly* 20, May 1977.

P/3 Technology

Articles and reports

336. Bartolic, L (1975) Technical English: a method of teaching the cause-effect relation as applied to a diagram *ELT Journal* 29, 2, January 1975.
337. Bodley, J (1977) English on site: checking results *IUT Bulletin Pédagogique* November 1977.
338. Candlin, C N, and D Murphy (1976) *Engineering discourse and listening comprehension*. A report. University of Lancaster.
339. Coleman, Hywel (1976) Teaching English in the Petroleum Industry *Petroleum English Bulletin* No 1, December 1976.
340. Coleman, Hywel (1977a) First intensive English course for staff of the Indonesian Petroleum Institute *Petroleum English Bulletin* 2, June 1977.
341. Coleman, Hywel (1977b) P T Arun's in-service language training workshop *Petroleum English Bulletin* 2, June 1977.
342. Coutts, Jennifer (1974) Industrial language training *Audio-Visual Language Journal* 12, 1.
343. Coveney, J (1974) 'French for engineers', in Perren (*ed*) (1974) (66).
344. Coveney, J (1975) The teaching of languages to technologists *System* 3, 2.
345. Drobnic, Karl (1978) Teaching conceptual paragraphs in EST courses – a practical technique *ESPMENA Bulletin* 10, Spring 1978.
346. Fitzgerald, M (1977) Industrial language training, in Holden (*ed*) (55).
347. Gorosch, M (1965) English in the industrial workshop *IRAL* 3, 4. Also in *IUT Bulletin Pédagogique* 8, June 1970.
348. Jones, T (1978) 'The foundation course in laboratory procedures at King

Faisal University Communication Skills in English Project', in British Council (1978a) (48).
349. Knowles, D (1976) Orientation and English language course for prospective gas field technicians *Petroleum English Bulletin* No 1, December 1976.
350. Mackay, R, and A Mountford (1978) 'A programme for postgraduate soil scientists at the University of Newcastle', in Mackay and Mountford (*eds*) (1978) (59).
351. Merle, Laurent (1972) A non-technician's attempts at some techniques for the technical *IUT Bulletin Pédagogique* February 1972.
352. Mintardi, B (1977) Planning English language courses for staff *Petroleum English Bulletin* 2, June 1977.
353. Phillips, M, C Shettlesworth, L Kerr, and S Denny (1974) Some linguistic and functional aspects of an English course for students in Agriculture. Paper delivered at the 4th annual seminar of the Association of Professors of English in Iran, 14th–17th March 1974. British Council, ETIC archives.
354. Root, A C (1972) Kingston–Cachan research project *IUT Bulletin Pédagogique* November 1972.
355. Shankland, W (1972) Technical English 'en direct' *IUT Bulletin Pédagogique* February 1972.
356. Sharma, Ram S (1978) The teaching of technical English in the Indian context *IRAL* 16, 2, May 1978.
357. Smith, M A (1977) Common sense and ESP: an industrial language training project *Petroleum English Bulletin* 2 June 1977.
358. Trimble, Louis, and R M Todd Trimble (1977) 'The development of EFL materials for occupational English', in British Council (1977) (47).
359. Ulijn, J M (1972) Foreign language needs at a Dutch university of technology *IUT Bulletin Pédagogique* June 1972.
360. Ulijn, J M (1978) French as a foreign language in Engineering education – an investigation into reading comprehension *Journal of Research in Reading* Eindhoven.
361. Yarmohammadi, L (1976) 'English–Persian language problems in technological and scientific subjects in Iran' British Council, ETIC archives.

Textbooks

362. Beardwood, L, H Templeton, and M Webber (1978) *A first course in technical English* Heinemann.
363. Blakey, T N (1978) *English for Maritime Studies* Edinburgh Language Foundation.
364. Brasnett, C (1969) *English for Engineers* Methuen.
365. Review of Brasnett (1969) by P Fanning, in *ESPMENA Bulletin* 9, 1977.
366. Broughton, G (1965a) *A first technical reader* Macmillan.

367. Broughton, G (1965b) *A technical reader for advanced students* Macmillan.
368. English Language Teaching Development Unit (1973) *English in flight* Oxford University Press.
369. English Language Teaching Development Unit (1974) *The Crisis Series* Oxford University Press.
370. Glendinning, Eric (1973) *English in Mechanical Engineering* (English in Focus Series) Oxford University Press.
371. Review of Glendinning (1973) by Lee Kok Cheong *RELC Journal* 7, 1, 1976.
372. Hawkey, M (1970) *English practice for Engineers* Longman.
373. Herbert, A J (1965) *The structure of technical English* Longman.
374. Hodlin, S, T C Jupp, and E Laird (1974) *English in the laundry. An English language training course for overseas staff in hospital laundries* The King's Fund Centre, 24 Nutford Place, London W1H 6AN.
375. Jupp, T C et al (1975) *Industrial English* Heinemann.
376. Review of Jupp, T C et al (1975) by James Crofts, *ESPMENA Bulletin* 5, Autumn 1976.
377. McAllister, J, and G Madama (1976) *English for Electrical Engineers* Longman.
378. Methold, K, and D D Waters (1973) *Understanding technical English* Longman.
379. Mountford, A (1975) *English in workshop practice* (English in Focus Series) Oxford University Press.
380. Review of Mountford (1975) by R A Knight, in *RELC Journal* 7, 1, 1976.
381. Mountford, A (1977) *English in Agriculture* (English in Focus Series) Oxford University Press.
382. Rossner, R, and J Taylor (1973) *Technical English reader 1 and 2* Macmillan.
383. Scott, J S (1969) *Civil Engineering. Technical English Supplementary Reader, 1* Longman.
384. Stacey, Richard *English for international switchboard operators* Mimeo. Polyglot, Manama, Bahrein (undated).
385. Wells, G W (1970) *Electronics and communications* (Technical English Supplementary Readers) Longman.

Packs
386. *North Sea challenge. Language Training Pack 1* Linguistics Systems Engineering/BP Educational Service.
387. *Tutor-Tape Audio-Visual Technical Series: E84 Engine Principles, E91 Tests of Petroleum Lubricants* Tutor-Tape, 258 Wimbledon Park Road, London SW19.

P/4 Medicine

Articles
388. Allwright, Joan, and Richard Allwright (1977). 'An approach to the teaching of medical English' in Holden (*ed*) (55).
389. Candlin, C N, C J Bruton, and J H Leather (1976a) Doctors in casualty: specialist course design from a data base *IRAL* 3.
390. Currie, W B, G Sturtridge, and J Allwright (1974) A technique of teaching medical English *Proceedings of the 3rd International Congress of Applied Linguistics* Groos, Heidelberg.
391. Edwards, Paula J (1974) Teaching specialist English (with special reference to English for nurses and midwives in Nigeria) *ELT Journal* 28, 3, April 1974.
392. Hadzi-Jovancic, D (1976) 'Certain rhetorical aspects of medical discourse', in Nickel (*ed*) *Proceedings of the 4th International Congress of Applied Linguistics* Stuttgart.
393. Harper, D P L (1974) 'English for foreign doctors and civil servants', in Perren (*ed*) (1974) (66).
394. Luceri, R, and R Duda (1975) A course in advanced medical English *Mélanges Pédagogiques* CRAPEL.
395. van Naerssen, Margaret M (1978) ESL in medicine: a matter of life and death *TESOL Quarterly* 12, 2, June 1972.

Textbooks
396. Austin, David, and Tim Crosfield (1976) *English for nurses* Longman.
397. Bloom, Gretchen (1976) *The language of hospital services in English* (English for Careers Series) Regents Publishing Company, New York.
398. Brasnett, Clive (1976) *English for medical students* Methuen.
399. Review of Brasnett (1976) by P Fanning, in *ESPMENA Bulletin* 9, 1977.
400. Candlin, C N, C J Bruton, J H Leather, and E G Woods *DOPACS: Doctor-patient communication skills* University of Lancaster/Medical Recording Service Foundation (undated).
401. Horzella, Maria, and Angela Labarca (1974) *English for Medicine* Mimeo. University of Chile.
402. Maclean, Joan (1975) *English in basic Medical Science* (English in Focus Series) Oxford University Press.
403. Review of Maclean (1975) by P Fanning, and J Swales in *ESPMENA Bulletin* 3, 1975.
404. Review of Maclean (1975) by J Honeyfield, in *RELC Journal* 7, 1, 1976.
405. Methold, K, and C Methold (1975) *Practice in medical English* Longman.
406. Review of Methold and Methold (1975) by Paul Fanning, in *ESPMENA Bulletin* 4, Spring 1976.

407. Parkinson, Joy (1976) *A manual of English for the overseas Doctor* Churchill Livingstone/Longman.
408. Parkinson, Joy (1978) *English for doctors and nurses* Evans.
409. Swales, J (1979) *English for the medical laboratory* Nelson.
410. Thomas, D, and J Thomas (1969) *English for nurses* Edward Arnold.

P/5 Commerce

Articles

411. Bianchi, Mary (1973) 'The selection of linguistic material for the VHS Certificate "English for Business purposes" ', in de Grève *et al* (*eds*) (54).
412. Castely, A J (1977) Some aspects of foreign language courses for business people *Modern Languages* 58, 2, June 1977.
413. Chromecka, J (1974) The teaching of English in factory institutes *ELT Journal* 28, 2, January 1974.

Textbooks

414. Beesley, Alan R (1971) *English for your business career Bks 1 and 2* Collier-Macmillan. Book 3 with Philip Bedford Robinson.
415. Binham, Philip (1968) *Executive English. Books 1 and 2* Longman.
416. BBC (1973) *English for business: The Bellcrest file* BBC/Oxford University Press.
417. BBC (1976) *Modern Office Ltd* BBC/Oxford University Press.
418. Coles, Michael and Basil Lord (1970) *Colloquial English* Oxford University Press.
419. Coles, Michael, and Basil Lord (1973) *The Savoy English course* Edward Arnold.
420. Conrad, Louis (1973) *Let's talk business* Geoffrey Chapman.
421. Costinett, S (1978) *The language of Accounting in English* (English for Careers Series) Regents Publishing Company, New York.
422. Educational Services (1954) *Commercial correspondence for students of English as a Second Language* McGraw-Hill.
423. English Language Teaching Development Unit (1972) *Accounting in English. Programmed units* Oxford University Press.
424. English Language Teaching Development Unit (1974a) *The Case of Harkwood Ltd* Oxford University Press.
425. English Language Development Unit (1974b) *English for secretaries* Oxford University Press.
426. English Language Teaching Development Unit (1976) *State your case* Oxford University Press.
427. English Language Teaching Development Unit (1978) *The visit* Oxford University Press.

428. Ferguson, N, and M O'Reilly (1978a) *English for bank cashiers* Evans.
429. Ferguson, N, and M O'Reilly (1978b) *English for International Banking* Evans.
430. Fisher, David (1968) *Commercial English comprehension passages* Longman.
431. Heyworth, Frank (1978) *Language of discussion* Hodder & Stoughton.
432. Howatt, Anthony, John Webb, and Michael Knight (1975) *A Modern Course in Business English* Oxford University Press.
433. Kench, A B (1972) *The language of English business letters* Macmillan.
434. Knight, Michael, and Bea Woolrich (1967) *English at work* Longman.
435. Mack, Angela (1970) *The language of business* BBC Publications.
436. Mavor, W Ferrier (1971) *English for business* Pitman.
437. Moore, B (1979) *English for the office* Macmillan.
438. Naidoo, P, M Bolch, and M Walker (1971) *Office practice. Book 1: clerical duties* (Special English Series) Collier-Macmillan.
439. Naidoo, P, and M Bolch (1971) *Office practice. Book 2: secretarial duties* (Special English Series) Collier-Macmillan.
440. Naterop, B, E Weis, and E Haberfellner (1977) *Business letters for all* Oxford University Press, Kuala Lumpur.
441. O'Neill R (1976) *Business news* Longman.
442. O'Reilly, M, P E Moran, and N Ferguson (1975) *Talking Business* Macmillan.
443. Parsons, C J (1977) *Problems in business communications* Edward Arnold.
444. Parsons, C J, and S J Hughes *Written communication for business students* Edward Arnold.
445. Pearson, Christopher (1975) *Getting down to business in English. Books 1 and 2* Heinemann.
446. Robinson, Philip (1977) *Import/Export* (Special English Series) Collier-Macmillan.
447. de Schiffrin, R S, B A Uteda, and E J Golskin (1969) *English in Action* Longman.
448. Spooner, M D, and J S McKellan (1975) *Commercial correspondence in English* Nelson.
449. Spooner, M D, and J S McKellan (1978) *Practical business letters* Nelson.
450. Stanwell, S, and M Swift (1978) *English in the office. Book 1* Edward Arnold.
451. Woolcott, L A, and W R Unwin (1974) *Communication for business and secretarial students* Macmillan.

Packs

452. *Q-Cards: The parent-teacher meeting, The budget meeting, The creditors' meeting.* Paul Norbury Publications Ltd.

P/6 Study skills

Articles and reports

453. Candlin, C N, J M Kirkwood, and M M Moore (1975) 'Developing study skills in English', in British Council (1975) (44).
454. Candlin, C N, J M Kirkwood, and H M Moore (1978) 'Study skills in English: theoretical issues and practical problems', in Mackay and Mountford *(eds)* (1978) (59).
455. Central Institute of English, Hyderabad (1965) ' "Sandwich" vocabulary for engineering students' British Council, ETIC archives.
456. Chamberlain, R G D, and M K S Flanagan (1978) 'Developing a flexible ESP programme design', in British Council (1978a) (48).
457. Cleary, J (1978) 'The use of video-tape recordings on the communication skills in English Project, KAAV', in British Council (1978a) (48).
458. Cowie, A P (1977) 'Teaching academic writing within a functional perspective: the problem of methodology'. Paper delivered at the BAAL ESP Seminar, Bath.
459. Douglas, D (1977) *From school to university. The Study Habits Research Project Final Report* University of Khartoum Students' Affairs Section.
460. Freeman, S (1976) 'Some ways of tackling the change to English-medium instruction at tertiary level. With a battery of exercises as training for note-taking from lectures' British Council, ETIC archives. Also in *Modern English Teacher* 6, 5, 1978.
461. Greenall, G M (1978) 'Designing Science writing materials', in British Council (1978a) (48).
462. Herbolich, J B (1978) Teaching outlining to the ESP student *ESPMENA Bulletin* 10, Spring 1978.
463. Holes, C D (1972) *An investigation into some aspects of the English language problems of two groups of overseas post-graduate students at Birmingham University*. MA thesis, University of Birmingham.
464. Johns, T F (1975) Seminar discourse strategies: problems and principles in role simulation *ELT Documents* 75/3. British Council.
465. Johns, T F, and C M Johns (1976) 'The current programme of materials development in English for Academic Purposes at the Universities of Aston and Birmingham', in Richards *(ed)* (67).
466. Jordan, R R (1977) 'English for Academic Purposes: Economics', in Johnson *(ed)* (56).
467. Jordan, R R (1978) 'Language practice materials for economists', in Mackay and Mountford *(eds)* (1978) (59).
468. Jordan, R R, and A Matthews (1978) 'English for Academic Purposes: practice material for the listening comprehension and writing needs of overseas students', in British Council (1978a) (48).
469. KAAU ESP Research Project (1976) *The structure of lectures. Final report*. University of Birmingham.

470. King, P (1978) 'The CSE Programme for medical students at KAAU and the Science or language dilemma', in British Council (1978a) (48).
471. Lilley, A D (1976) 'Towards the analysis of a communicative situation: the Science lecture' British Council, ETIC archives.
472. McDonough, J E English for Academic Purposes: some factors in listening comprehension *Lenguas para Objectivos Especificos* Cuaderno 4 (undated).
473. Mackay, R, and A Mountford (1974) Reading for information. Paper presented at the 9th Regional Seminar, Singapore. British Council, ETIC archives.
474. Martin, A V (1976) Teaching academic vocabulary to foreign graduate students *TESOL Quarterly* 10, 1, March 1976.
475. Moody, K W (1976) A type of exercise for developing prediction skills reading *RELC Journal* 7, 1, June 1976.
476. Montgomery, M M (1976) *The linguistic structure of lectures*. MLitt thesis, University of Birmingham.
477. Morrison, J (1978) Designing a course in advanced listening comprehension in Mackay and Mountford (eds) (1978) (59).
478. Plaister, T (1973) Teaching reading comprehension to the advanced ESL student using the cloze procedure. *RELC Journal* 4, 2, December 1973.
479. Sharwood-Smith, M (1976) New directions in teaching written English *English Teaching Forum* 14, 2, April 1976.
480. Straker-Cook, R (1978) 'A "social survival" syllabus', in Mackay and Mountford (eds) (1978) (59).
481. Sullivan, E (1976) 'Listening tapes': preparing for university lectures *English Teaching Forum* 14, 3, July 1976.
482. Wijasuriya, B S (1971) *The occurrence of discourse markers and intersentence connectives in university lectures and their place in the testing and teaching of listening comprehension in EFL*. MEd thesis, University of Manchester.

Textbooks

483. Candlin, C N, J M Kirkwood, and H M Moore (1976) *Study skills in English* University of Lancaster.
484. Cooper, J (1979) *Think and link. An advanced course in reading and writing skills* Edward Arnold.
485. Ferguson, N, and M O'Reilly (1978) *Listening and note-taking* Evans.
486. Heaton, J B (1975) *Studying in English* Longman.
487. Review of Heaton, J B (1975) by T Bex in *ESPMENA Bulletin* 9, Winter 1977–78.
488. Review of Heaton (1975) by G R Esary in *RELC Journal* 8, 1, 1977.
489. James, K, R R Jordan, and A J Matthews (1979) *Listening comprehension and note-taking course* Collins.

490. Plaister, T (1976) *Developing listening comprehension for ESL Students: The Kingdom of Kochen* Englewood Cliffs, Prentice-Hall, NJ.
491. Review of Plaister (1976) by C Smith in *TESOL Quarterly* 11, 2, 1977.
492. Purvis, K (1978) *Read and note. English study skills for Science and Medicine* Heinemann.
493. Review of Purvis (1978) by P Wingard in *ESPMENA Bulletin* 11.
494. *Reading and thinking in English* (1979) Oxford University Press.
495. Wallace, M (1979) *Study skills in English* Cambridge University Press.
496. Yorkey, R C (1976) *Study skills for students of English as a Second Language* McGraw-Hill.
497. Review of Yorkey (1976) by B Matthies in *TESOL Quarterly* 6, 2, 1972.
498. Review of Yorkey (1971) by G R Esarey in *RELC Journal* 8, 1, 1977.

Packs

499. McDonough, J (1978) *Listening to Lectures* A series of cassettes and workbooks on extracts from authentic lectures. Subject areas covered so far are *Computing, Biology, Government, Mechanics, Sociology*. Oxford University Press.

P/7 Other

500. Booth, A, and T Hashimoto (1978) *Let's see Europe* Macmillan.
501. Case, D, and P Snow (1976) *Take a break. The English you need for travel* BBC.
502. Chamberlin, D, and G White (1976) *English for translation* Cambridge University Press.
503. Ferguson, N, and M O'Reilly (1978d) *English telephone conversations* Evans.
504. Roe, P (1976) *English for international cooperation* BBC.